PRIVATE DEVELOPMENT AID IN TRANSITION

About the Authors

Fons van der Velden is director of 'Context, International Cooperation' (research, advice and training) in Utrecht, the Netherlands and Head of the Post-Graduate Course Development Studies of the Centre for International Development Issues Nijmegen (University of Nijmegen, the Netherlands). He has done extensive fieldwork in India and numerous assignments in sub-Saharan Africa. He is the (co-) author of several publications about Dutch private investments and foreign aid, including Regional Development and the International Division of Labour, also published by Concept Publishing Company.

Lau Schulpen defended his PhD thesis entitled The Same Difference - A Comparative Analysis of Dutch Aid Channels to India in 1997. Afterwards he continued his work as lecturer/researcher at the Centre for International Development Issues Nijmegen (University of Nijmegen, the Netherlands). In recent years he has conducted (further) research in such fields as poverty reduction (mainly India), partnership, and private sector development. Presently he is, among other things, involved in research concerning the role of non-governmental development organisations within civil society in India.

PRIVATE DEVELOPMENT AID IN TRANSITION

FONS VAN DER VELDEN
and
LAU SCHULPEN

Editor
MARIANNE WIJERMARS

CONCEPT PUBLISHING COMPANY, NEW DELHI-110059

The views and opinions expressed in this report are those of the authors and do not necessarily reflect the views of the organization to which they belong.

ISBN-81-7022-947-2

First Published 2002

Published and Printed by
Ashok Kumar Mittal
Concept Publishing Company
A/15-16, Commercial Block, Mohan Garden
NEW DELHI-110059 (India)

Phones : 5648039, 5649024
Fax : 091-11-5648053
E-mail : publishing@conceptpub.com

FOREWORD

Political institutions and economic systems have never converged across nation states more sharply than during this millennium. The speed at which technological advancement has been changing social relations – primarily economic relations and ultimately political relations – is unprecedented.

The history of human civilisation has always been marked by evolutionary and revolutionary processes – 'inventions and discoveries' – that have changed its course dramatically. Whether it be electricity, the steam engine, nuclear energy, the discovery of new continents or space ships landing on the moon – all of them had a big hand in influencing civilisation. The impact of changes wrought by the industrial revolution can be felt even today. Hitherto comprising of merchant guilds, the economy now turned to industrial modes of production. The political system transcended from monarchy to parliamentary democracy. Concepts such as liberty, equality and fraternity gave birth to ideologies that shaped economic as well as political institutions.

The industrial revolution accelerated two streams of ideologies – with innumerable shades between them – which polarised the world: one, propagating the freedom of the individual (*lassez faire*), and the other, advocating concentration of power in the state (totalitarian state). The shift from the city-state politics of Athens to the modern form of parliamentary democracy saw the rise of several other forms of political systems – oligarchy, anarchy, monarchy, theocracy, dictatorship and democracy.

During the medieval period inventions, technological advancements and oceanic voyages led to expansion of trade that crossed geographical boundaries. In order to protect their trade interests the rulers used military power and, gradually, colonisation completed the political transfer of power from the natives to invaders. Thus, a historical perspective reveals the cultural domination and subjugation of colonised people by the colonisers using military power in order to protect the colonisers' economic interests. In short, colonisation was a by-product of inventions, discoveries and technological development leading to trade and invariably resulting in war.

The adage that 'history repeats itself' has never been more true. The digital and microchip revolutions and space technology have transformed communication systems across the world. When this technology was applied to trade, boundaries of nation states became anachronistic. GATT and WTO – instruments of the global village – have set in motion new forms of colonisation similar to that of the eighteenth century, the difference being that remote controls and satellite communications have made human presence (the erstwhile colonial ruler) redundant. And as this newer form of cultural dominance becomes more and more entrenched, it makes conflicts inevitable. Today, when we review development cooperation in a historical framework, we cannot overlook the fact that it is a post-world war phenomenon, arising out of the historical compulsions of cold war politics.

The so-called development decades were dominated by the race for nuclear power and proxy wars that dictated the geo-political equilibrium of strategic regions. The disintegration of the USSR set the stage for world capitalism and newer concepts of global governance. Therefore, the emerging forms of global systems, whether in the sphere of economic relations, politics or knowledge, are a culmination of inventions, discoveries and technological revolutions that act as 'drivers' for trade. Political ideologies, which owe allegiance to economic interests that promote neo-liberal economic models, and modernisation theories that are situated in the WTO regime, are skewed to protect the interests of multinational corporations of Northern governments. In such a context, the power of the state is gradually reduced in the Southern hemisphere, allowing trade by Northern groups to have freer movement, and making it possible for the knowledge systems and natural resources of the Southern hemisphere to be patented by North and resold to South. More than ever before, the responsibility of the state towards its own subjects is being withdrawn in the name of 'structural reforms' and 'conditionalities' dictated by international financial institutions.

With the integration of the Eastern block into the global economy, the framework for development assistance has changed drastically. This is reflected in the sharp fall in development assistance. Given this background, non-governmental development organisations (NGDOs), both in the North and the South, are perplexed and ambivalent about their role vis-à-vis the 'Market' and the 'State'.

Poverty, discrimination, denial of human rights and the struggle for survival are not novel experiences. But some nation states in the so-called 'global village' are becoming more prone to create conditions favouring the prosperity and affluence of one section of subjects, leaving large sections of the poor exposed to conditions that are unfavourable to their survival and security – the dichotomous nature of globalisation. The Northern states are thus gaining greater control over global resources. This exploitation by the North is effected primarily by using their economic and political power within the UN system, secondly as collective syndicates, and thirdly by forging alliances with those who can 'further their interests' – military, strategic and economic. Thus, we have the G7 nations, the elite nuclear club, the Euro-Dollar single currency strategy, etcetera.

Viewed in such a context, development assistance is not value neutral; it advocates and perpetuates, implicitly and explicitly, development paradigms that are favourable to the country that provides aid. Development cooperation by Northern NGDOs therefore has already become part of a dominant system, making all programmatic or policy frameworks they may evolve subservient to the larger system. The personnel, who implement development cooperation, are part of the cultural system as individuals and as members of an organisation. The corresponding organisations in the South are so divergent in their worldviews, development ideologies and development approaches, that they end up pursuing the means more vigorously than the end. This is subtly brought out in this book – the dominant paradigm led by the 'New Policy Agenda'. The Northern NGDOs' contradictions are aptly portrayed as a midlife crisis. The Southern NGDOs, whose 'golden age' is on the decline, are confronted with innumerable problems that appear to be insurmountable. What, then, does the future hold for the NGDOS and the poor, for countries where the poor live in large numbers? For those who want to alleviate and eradicate their poverty? And for those who want to contribute to this process? There are far reaching questions raised from a cultural perspective as to how one uses power: over resources and ideology to perpetuate dominant development paradigms.

The book focuses on a single country, a single NGDO from the North, and reviews it both from the viewpoint of the country in which the NGDO originates and from the perspective of a global framework of development assistance on the one hand and micro action at project level in one country, i.e., India, on the other. What comes through powerfully is the complexity of the poverty issue, with all its ramifications of social, political, economic, cultural and international relations. Organisational and strategic dimensions add to the limited scope of 'development cooperation' by private development NGDOs in their present form. The book does not pretend to offer prescriptions or solutions. What it does provide is a range of questions and insights: how strategic development cooperation has been either by Northern or Southern NGDOs; the absence of horizontal links between Northern NGDOs on the one hand and between the government and NGDOs on the other; the long-term implications of development cooperation in a country by an NGDO, did the organisational history (ICCO) of five decades of development cooperation create a learning organisation? What myths have been created and perpetuated? What organisational cultures were created? Did they manage to transcend cross-cultural complexities?

The need for systematic empirical studies and greater exchange of ideas and insights between the various stakeholders is critical for development cooperation. The authors' emphasis on culture and its relevance and significance in the context of development is very heartening as this aspect is often overlooked by Western authorship. Lastly, development cooperation needs to be based on Southern perspectives and cultural frames that are not reductionist but generative, not single dimensional but multi-dimensional, not perpetuated by myths but based on facts, not mono-polar but pluralistic, not dominant but interdependent.

The role of the state cannot be minimised. Despite thousands of NGDOs performing at their optimum levels of efficiency, whether in the South or in the North, poverty cannot be eradicated as long as structural inequities exist in the South and between the North and the South. Poverty reduction strategies thus need to take into account the larger canvas and evolve models of cooperation between multiple stakeholders. However, the advocacy vis-à-vis the market in the North would play a critical role in consolidating development gains in the South.

F. STEPHEN
SEARCH, Bangalore

September 2001

CONTENTS

PART IV: NGDOS: CHALLENGES FOR THE FUTURE

PART - I

INTRODUCTION

1

THE RISE AND FALL OF NORTHERN NGDOs?

— *Fons van der Velden*

In the last decades the role of non-governmental development organisations (NGDOs) in development aid has increased significantly. For a long period the functioning of Northern NGDOs, the impact and effectiveness of their activities, and their relationships with Southern counterparts were hardly examined or criticised. In recent years, however, this has changed.

Development cooperation

Present day international development cooperation should be analysed in its historical context. One of the consequences of the economic depression of the 1930s and the ensuing Second World War was the decline of the leading position of the United Kingdom in the world economy. That role was taken over by the United States, which turned out to be well prepared for the position (Bol, 1978). From post-war planning it is obvious that the international economic order was supposed to satisfy three fundamental American interests: access to the raw materials and minerals of the Southern countries, the creation of consumer markets adequate to absorb American products and services, and the creation of investment possibilities in the former colonies if and when this was required by lack of internal investment opportunities (Kolko, 1972).

Against this background the Bretton Woods institutions were created, i.e. the International Monetary Fund (IMF) and the

International Bank for Reconstruction and Development (IBRD). Moreover, the United States stimulated the establishment of the General Agreement on Trade and Tariffs (GATT) (Nissen, 1975; Payer, 1975). Other manifestations of this international policy were the Marshall Plan for the post-war reconstruction of Europe, and the plan for development cooperation. According to the Dutch development economist Dick Bol: 'With the Marshall Plan a model of intergovernmental aid was created which had very little to do with generosity. The donor could derive appreciable advantages from the aid relation, advantages which had no direct relationship with the volume of the assistance' (Bol, 1978: 67).

It is therefore justified to put the beginning of development cooperation at the inauguration speech of Harry S. Truman in which, for the first time, the Southern hemisphere was defined as 'underdeveloped areas'. As Wolfgang Sachs pointed out: 'The label stuck and subsequently provided the cognitive base for both arrogant interventionism from the North and pathetic self-pity in the South' (Sachs, 1992: 2). Development aid, later renamed development cooperation, remains to this day a very important tool of foreign policy, not only in the United States but in most other OECD countries[1] . As Noam Chomsky, for one, declares: The Conquest Continues (Chomsky, 1993).[2]

In the post-war period, next to bilateral and multilateral government-level cooperation with Southern countries, a broad range of private development organisations were created in the North: non-governmental development organisations (NGDOs). They are generally non-commercial and non-profit oriented (Shah, 1991)[3]. NGDOs can be categorised in different ways. Firstly, organisations subsidised and/or recognised by a national government or multilateral institutions such as the European Union. Some examples are: Christian Aid in the United Kingdom; the Catholic organisation Cordaid (formerly CEBEMO), the ecumenical organisation ICCO, Hivos (humanistic) and Novib (basically social democratic) in the Netherlands; Evangelische

Zentralstelle für Entwicklungshilfe (EZE) and Brot für die Welt in Germany; and NCOS in Belgium. Secondly, according to their origin, for example churches, trade unions, women's organisations and humanitarian institutions. Thirdly, along the line of their main activities, e.g., environment, women and development, education. And finally, of course, according to ideological convictions (Kruijt et al., 1983). Ideologically, the private development community comprises, from its early days on, a wide range of different groups, institutions and individuals. Within this community there is certainly no unequivocal standpoint with regard to development cooperation. Opinions vary from an unconditional plea for more assistance to a complete rejection of any type of assistance (see also Chapter 6).

Although a number of private institutions depend strongly on national governments or international establishments, they do, in practice, command an appreciable autonomy, especially those with charity funds. This relative independence may lead to more room for manoeuvre, and more possibilities to achieve a qualitative change in their relationships with counterpart organisations in the South[4].

In the last ten years the non-governmental development sector worldwide has undergone major changes. NGDOs have mushroomed in many countries in the South, Eastern Europe as well as in the North.[5] At some international conferences NGDO meetings attract more attention than the official meetings (UNCED, Rio de Janeiro, 1992; UN Conference on Women, Beijing, 1995). The increase of financial means made available through this channel is another expression of the growing recognition of the work done by NGDOs. During the period 1970-1990 funds increased threefold to 13 per cent of all OECD government aid (Fowler, 1992; UNDP, 1993: 93). Internationally, the growing significance of the NGDO sector is reflected in the recognition and appreciation of multilateral organisations such as the OECD, World Bank, UNICEF and, in particular, UNDP (Smillie & Helmich, 1994; UNDP, 1993; World Bank, 1988; World Bank, 1990a). Nowadays participation of the poor is seen as an important prerequisite for the successful implementation of development projects.[6] UNDP's Human Development Report 1993, which focuses on participation and elaborates extensively on the important role of NGDOs, could be seen as a culmination of this trend. The 1993 Report pleads for the need 'to decentralize more authority to local governments and to give much greater freedom to people's organisations and non-governmental organisations' (UNDP, 1993: 5). In the words of Oakly, participation is seen 'as the key to the inclusion of human resources in development efforts' (Oakly, 1994: 2).[7]

In the Dutch development community NGDOs play an important role in different areas as well (financing development activities, lobbying and advocacy, development education in the Netherlands) and this role has increasingly been appreciated by the government. For instance, in the period 1980-1998 the funds provided by the government for co-financing rose from NLG 241 million to NLG 677 million (Haijtink & Hoebink, 1998: 99). The percentage of the budget allocated to the four co-financing organisations (Bilance [now Cordaid], Hivos, ICCO and Novib) has increased considerably in recent years.

The intrinsic value of NGDOs is demonstrated in their ability to reach the poorest of the poor directly, their contribution to poverty reduction, and, particularly in recent years, community development, the granting of credit, emancipation of marginal groups, putting the issue of sex-based discrimination on the agenda, and the implementation of emergency aid programmes (Pronk, 1990: 309; Van der Velden, 1980; UNDP, 1993, in particular Chapter V). Moreover, IMF's neo-liberal adjustment programmes call for privatisation, and hence a bigger participation of NGDOs in the provision of basic needs such as health care and education, and in general the implementation of developmental activities for poor and marginalised groups.

Summarised, it may be stated that politically, with regard to policy, and from a public relations point of view, aid provided through private channels to similar organisations and institutions in the South plays an important role in the debate on the objectives, the effectiveness and the efficiency of development cooperation with Southern countries.

Dilemmas at the implementation level

Over the years Northern NGDOs have made a substantial (financial) contribution to poverty alleviation projects and programmes of private development organisations in the South, as well as to the dialogue between like-minded organisations and institutions in the South and the North.

At the same time it should be acknowledged that in practice private development organisations from the North face a number of dilemmas, paradoxes and problems, both in the implementation of their activities and, in particular, in the shaping of their relationships with their counterpart organisations in the South.[8] The problems may differ widely in level and complexity but they put a strain on the functioning of the organisations concerned and their staff (Van der Velden, 1994a). Below, the most important dilemmas will be summarised.

Dilemma 1: Aid does not work

First and foremost, development experts face the problem that over the last decade little progress has been made in the fight against poverty.[9] Aid does not work, or not sufficiently, as a counterpoint to the impoverishment that takes place within countries and between countries.

It is true that, according to UNDP, the percentage of people worldwide living in absolute poverty decreased between 1970 and 1985. However, as a consequence of unfavourable conditions of the world economy and planning processes in the developing countries themselves their number increased by about one fifth in the same period (UNDP, 1990).

Development cooperation is a relatively marginal activity in relations between countries.[10] About 14 per cent of the total official development assistance (ODA) is channelled through private organisations. With this aid, about one per cent of the population can be reached (Hardeman et al., 1993; Tims, 1995). Moreover, the total flow of ODA has stagnated since the 1980s: 'a long feared stagnation and perhaps even decline in total ODA from DAC member countries may have begun' (United Nations, 1995: 129-130).

In the first place, it must be recognised, as is done among others by the World Bank and Cassen et al. (1994), that from a macro-economic point of view there is no clear and direct relation between development cooperation and development. Aid seems to be only one of the factors which play a role in development.[11]

In the second place, the effectiveness of private cooperation leaves much to be desired. The outcome of various studies suggests that only in 50 per cent of cases the investment can be considered appropriate and effective (Jepma, 1995; Schulpen & Van der Velden, 1992; Ridell & Robinson, 1992).

Of course, this does not mean that in specific cases and/or at the micro-level private development cooperation cannot be of the utmost importance. Everyone who has travelled in Africa, Asia or Latin America must have seen the 'flowers in the dust' which have improved the socio-economic situation and increased the political resistance of the poor in certain regions (Teerink *et al.,* 1991; Hoebink, 1995). The fact remains, however, that from a macro-economic point of view international development cooperation, and in particular development cooperation from the private sector, is relatively unimportant.

Dilemma 2: The 'poorest of the poor'

'In 1988 about 41 per cent of foreign aid went to countries with a moderate and even high level of national income, essentially for political reasons. The aid per head of the population, which was offered, varied appreciably from country to country and it is quite certain that the poorest countries did not receive the largest part of the aid' (World Bank, 1992). This is equally true for private development aid.

In Rural Development : Putting the last first and in later publications Robert Chambers shows that the same mechanism can be observed within countries. Remote regions and the poorest of the poor (mostly women, children and old people) are very often neither noticed nor offered assistance by outsiders (Chambers, 1983; Chambers, 1985).

Here we deal with one of the major dilemmas in development cooperation: the poorest countries and regions lack the infrastructure to absorb foreign aid. Typical of the 'poorest of the poor' (the most important target group of the private sector) is that they are not organised, have no well-defined place of residence and whereabouts and can therefore not easily be reached through the often inflexible channels which are used by funding organisations. Moreover, in general most programmes are directed at males and at those who possess land. As a result, the upper-poor and middle class benefit most of private development aid (Van der Velden, 1980, especially Chapter 4).

Dilemma 3: Paternalism

Private development organisations, in general, have highly dedicated staff with a strong community spirit (Wils, 1991). However, and this must also be said, this strong commitment of the staff may lead to problems with regard to 'detachment and involvement'. It may result in the predominance of the development paradigm that is prevalent in the North. Yash Tandon in this context remarks that 'Europeans tend to regard their own value system as being universally valid' (Tandon, 1993: 127; see also Barrez, 1993).

The often very intense interference by donors may have as a result that 'a project is redefined in the financing phase to such an extent that the changes in objectives, methods and execution phases drastically change the nature of the project as well' (Elizalde, 1993:168). As a consequence, people responsible for the implementation may not recognise themselves in the project which has been forced upon them.

'Do-gooders' in the private organisations are not the only ones guilty of such practices. International institutions like the World Bank, IMF and the European Union often have the same attitude. In those cases, however, we do not speak about a 'missionary goodwill attitude' but about the safeguarding of Northern political and economical interests (Chomsky, 1993; Fowler, 1994).

In general, there is a growing tendency in international development cooperation to impose more (and more stringent) conditions on the provision of financial assistance (Clayton, 1994). This foreign interference is increasingly opposed by the countries from the South, and especially by representatives of development organisations. Some years ago several African representatives made it abundantly clear that they have had more than enough of the paternalism of the (private) development cooperation organisations. 'Sometimes you give the aid which you think we need, but you do not give us the help which we want' (Buchi Emecheta). Rakiya Omaar: 'NGOs do as much harm as they do good. They deny Africans a say in what happens in their own country'. She called this philanthropic imperialism (Evers *et al.*, 1993: 6 & 14).

Dilemma 4 : Semantics of cooperation

Multilateral as well as bilateral and private development cooperation use specific semantics. The base for this was laid in the so-called Pearson Report, entitled Partners in Progress which was published in 1969 by the then chairman of the World Bank. Development aid was redefined as development cooperation between equal partners, thus giving the impression that these partners work in a politico-economical vacuum.

Equally, most of the private development organisations talk about their counterparts in the South as partners or partner organisations. Other manifestations of this trend are phrases like round table conference, partner dialogue, sharing of resources and resource sharing agencies.

This representation is not always in accordance with the actual situation. Cooperation is often covered with an ideological blanket, which makes it difficult to analyse the (institutional) differences and recognise actual realities within these relationships. Also, within private development organisations one can observe the relationship between aid and power and often a 'monologue-ised dialogue' (Barrez, 1993; Sizoo (ed.), 1993).

Dilemma 5: Intermediate or primary organisations?

From the time when private channels were first employed, one of the most important presuppositions was that through direct contact with groups in the Third World the poorest of the poor could be reached efficiently and effectively. Private organisations cooperate with a multitude of different counterparts. Direct contact between financing agencies in the North and primary organisations does not occur very often (Steering Group Impact Co-financing Programme, 1991).

The above-mentioned presupposition proves to be the Achilles heel of private development cooperation. It turns out to be a myth that Northern organisations are in direct contact with 'low-opportunity' target groups. Normally, these groups are only contacted by intermediary organisations in developing countries that request funding from Northern donor agencies. These intermediary organisations do not by definition represent the aforementioned low-opportunity target groups. As a matter of fact the viewpoints of the requesting organisations are not necessarily identical with the real problems as seen by the poor themselves (Van Wichelen, 1978). Moreover, in a number of countries a tremendous mushrooming of NGDOs has taken place; in some countries government officials who were laid off during downsizing of bureaucracies under Structural Adjustment Programmes subsequently resurfaced as heads of newly-established NGDOs applying for funds from Northern NGDOs. In a number of such cases, running an NGDO has become merely another income-generating activity.

There is also a tendency to support an increasing number of organisations which form part of the so-called civil society. As a rule, this concerns intermediate organisations. While maturing, these organisations tend to remove from those they are supposed to represent. Professionalism coupled with a certain degree of institutionalisation can be functional. However, it can also result in a situation where the continued existence of the organisation coupled with the employment of the staff becomes an objective in itself which may gradually, at least in part, replace the objective of serving the needs of the poor.

Dilemma 6 : Overfunding

Practically, all private development organisations are under severe pressure to spend their funds within a certain period of time. This may arise from agreements with the government, the coupling of turnover and operating costs, pressure from benefactors and/or the danger of negative publicity in the case of underspending.

However, 'good' projects are generally difficult to find, and, more often than not, need only additional financing from abroad. Also, there is fierce competition among donors in practically all markets. This applies especially to projects which for the donors are 'non-labour intensive' and have a large absorption capacity.

Because of this spending pressure, requests from counterpart organisations are sometimes less critically judged, in particular at the end of the financial year. Aeroplanes, medicine in bulk, real estate and the donation of capital to counterpart organisations are not uncommon under these conditions.

There is also the problem of overfinancing. In the jargon it is sometimes said that an organisation is 'financed to pieces'. This generally happens when too many donors provide too much money in too short a time given the absorption capacity of the organisation and the target group. Staff with generally good managerial capabilities are often unable to cope with the profusion and the consequences are predictable. 'Easy money' often has a negative effect.[12]

Dilemma 7: Substitution

Although closely related to the preceding dilemma, separate mention should be made of the so-called substitution problem. African states in particular have been criticised for their inability to bring development to the people. In many African countries the state is in deep crisis and more or less discredited as an instrument for development (Dramé,1995; Tandon, 1993). The same is true for a number of countries in Asia and regions and groups in Latin America. As a consequence of the structural adjustment programmes imposed by IMF the local government is retreating from important service sectors in an increasing number of countries. Privatisation of development cooperation is on the increase worldwide.

Both funding organisations from the North and local NGDOs are tempted to accept these challenges: while helping the poor notable turnovers can be realised easily, and NGDOs are being heard and also appreciated by the public sector, the United Nations and the international financing institutions. This may be a manifestation of increasing democracy and willingness to take 'voices of the weaker sections' seriously.

Especially – but not only – in some African states more and more public services, such as health and education, are provided by local NGDOs. A well-known example is the provision of health services in Tanzania and Zimbabwe which, since the implementation of the Structural Adjustment Programme, are largely taken care of by private development organisations, especially church-based ones. In Bangladesh an NGDO is actively involved in the provision of primary education in a number of rural districts (Lewis, 1993).

Although in general the poor are not in a position to 'wait for Godot', the fundamental question remains whether the growing tendency to leave the provision of public services to NGDOs, and the civil society should be judged positively. Firstly, for ideological as well as practical reasons governments should remain responsible for providing these facilities; secondly, it is not desirable to set up a parallel system outside the government machinery; thirdly, in most cases NGDOs do not have the capability to take over this role; and finally, in view of the limited democratic character of these organisations, it cannot be considered desirable (Steering Group Impact Co-financing Programme, 1991).

Dilemma 8 : Quality or quantity?

Over the years a number of investigations have pointed out that attention to quality is of the utmost importance within private development cooperation (Quarles van Ufford et al., 1988). This attention should focus on the control of the quality of projects and programmes which are in the process of execution, as well as on policy. From a societal point of view there is an equally great demand for quality and control of quality of (private) development cooperation.

Endeavours to improve effectiveness are, however, often in contradiction with attempts to maximise the turnover. Private development organisations argue that funds are inadequate to achieve the objective of quality improvement. And indeed for the funding agencies, which are supported by governments or international agencies, overheads are a fixed percentage of the total turnover. This institutional constraint carries with it the danger that emphasis comes to be placed more on quantity than on quality. Lack of concern for quality, however, is more an attitude than a financial problem: it is quite possible to think of measures which can be taken in a budgetary neutral way (Van der Velden, 1994b).

Dilemma 9 : Image pressure

Similar to international agencies and governments, private development organisations tend to project a rather rosy picture of their activities. Realistic appraisals of the problems which the organisations encounter, both in the North and in the South, in the execution of the projects and programmes directed at the poor are hardly ever given. The public is even less likely to be informed about the situation of projects whose objectives are not reached. This problem arises particularly with organisations which generate their own funds, for instance Foster Parents/Plan International and Médecins sans Frontières.

This attitude has repercussions for activities directed at informing the public, and for development education programmes. More often than not the strategy is one of optimistic and positive representation.

For many reasons such a presentation is problematic. In the first place, a much too optimistic picture is created for the general public, a picture which does not coincide with reality and does not provide insights in the real problems processes of change in the South (Negash & Dejene, 1993). Moreover, this defensive strategy may lead to a decrease rather than a maintenance of support for development cooperation as less positive messages will reach the public through other channels.

In the second place, this often complacent presentation does not improve the ability of the private funding organisations to learn an ability which is sometimes rather limited anyhow. Based on a description of developments with regard to private development cooperation in a number of OECD countries, Ian Smillie puts forward: 'The importance of learning what works, and why, is essential to success. Knowing what does not work is even more important'. He regretfully remarks: 'The failure to learn from failure' sometimes seems to be much in evidence with financing organisations (Smillie & Helmich, 1994: 18-19).

Dilemma 10 : Overexposure of NGDO cooperation

The NGDO sector in the North sometimes seems to be a citadel under siege, with the enemy's fire coming from both the North and South. Also, internally, staff occasionally seem to be driven to desperation (Bossuyt, 1993).

However, some facts should not be overlooked. As discussed in the first dilemma, private development cooperation is only a small part of the international activity in this field. The limited number of empirical studies with regard to bilateral (Inspectie Ontwikkelingssamenwerking te Velde, 1994) and multilateral programmes certainly do not give the impression that the latter are more effective and efficient. For instance, the Operations Evaluation Department of the World Bank recently acknowledged that many Bank-financed operations were less than effective (cited in United Nations, 1995: 138). This is also one of the major findings of the Bank's assessment of its contribution to human development in sub-Saharan Africa (Ridker, 1994).

Finally, development cooperation should be considered in the total context of politico-economic relations. Excessive and disproportional attention to the private sector could lead attention away from the main issues.

Northern NGDO sector in crisis

Empirical evidence from other studies, such as the ODI/Institute of Development Studies about Finland, the ODI-studies about NGDOs from Great Britain and the study about the Belgian situation, confirm the observations made above (Achterhuis et al.,

1993; Ridell *et al.*, 1994; Ridell & Robinson, 1992; Farrington & Bebbington, 1993).[13]

Over the last few years, a number of development agencies in the North have commissioned evaluation and impact studies to analyse their performance. The outcome of these – often quite critical – studies has increased the speed with which agencies are trying to improve on their record. The emphasis thereby is on attempts to prove that their work is worthwhile; increasing the efficiency of the work; concentration on fewer counterpart organisations, countries and thematic issues; more cooperation among Northern agencies; and stronger emphasis on policy formulation, advocacy and political lobbying in the North (Lap, 1994).

However, it should be noted that these more or less managerial solutions, whereby the focus is mainly on controlling expenditure of funds and other supervisory measures, are inadequate to solve the most important problems. From various sides it has been emphasised that 'the responses made do not affect the relationships fundamentally' (Lap, 1994: 6). A critical observer from India comments almost cynically: 'Today the European agencies are taking a much more pragmatic approach to development... Maybe the Northern agencies are becoming efficient in management' (Stephen, 1994). In general, crisis management is currently prevalent in the aid sector in Western Europe (Hewitt, 1994).

It is no exaggeration to say that the NGDO sector in the North is experiencing a midlife crisis (Bossuyt, 1993). The situation is so serious that there is an urgent need for a thorough reflection on objectives, procedures and results (Van der Velden, 1994b).

Resistance to change

An important question is, of course, why the NGDOs in the North have not been able to cope with the above-mentioned problems related to their functioning and relationship with the counterpart organisation in the South. Some of the problems are as old as the road to Rome.

The inertia which works against dealing with these issues is most probably the result of three mutually related factors. In the first place, there are politico-economic causes. Alan Fowler once again emphasised that 'At the deepest level, growing governmental interest in supporting development in the South and East through NGOs stems from the economical and political ideology now dominating the global agenda – that of the market-led growth strategy and Western-style democracy' (Fowler, 1994). He states that today Northern governments can justify tax revenues for foreign aid, including subsidised private aid channels, 'if it facilitates the global replication of market capitalism by promoting trade and/or by mitigating negative effects of market expansion on poor and marginalised people which might induce their insurrection or an active search for a better life elsewhere'. According to Galbraith, in the present world order aid should contribute to global stability, reduce migration pressures and so on, in order to safeguard the life styles of 'contented' tax-paying Northern voters (Galbraith, 1992). Development cooperation, also through the private channels, should be used to part-finance a global system of social welfare for the Southern poor (Fowler, 1994).

Secondly, there is a solid resistance against change in the development bureaucracies in the North. Again, this results from the fact that the need for change is not, or at best hardly, recognised. Most probably the problem is that the current resource situation — of both the subsidised and fund raising agencies — is not 'hurting enough', and the idea that state funding, or funding through the 'charity market' is an entitlement for private development organisations, is deeply entrenched.[14] Moreover, it is very likely that the different organisations, due to their great geographical and psychological distance from the 'coal-front', hardly ever know what really happens to their funds in the field (Quarles van Ufford, 1995). The 'learn and adapt' capability is rather limited within the subsidised sector. Moreover, as said before, criticism is a politically sensitive subject. This has a paralysing effect on critical feedback from within.

Thirdly, the staff of development organisations are often themselves an important conservative factor. All too often (senior) staff members of funding agencies lack direct knowledge, and base their analysis and action on ignorance or on personal experience which is decades out of date (Chambers, 1992: 54; Sizoo, 1993). Moreover, relationships in development cooperation are, by definition, cultural relationships. Thus, a confrontation occurs between cultural patterns of choice. 'That is to say, that one's own value and behaviour patterns transpire not to be completely the same as that of the other – and implicitly or otherwise – are placed in question' (Sizoo, 1993: 25). This is difficult to deal with, as it creates uncertainty regarding one's own identity. The stronger the position of power one holds, the less one is inclined to allow discussion of this reaction. In quite a number of cases this leads to an authoritarian attitude vis à vis colleagues from the South in order to compensate for one's own uncertainty.

In other cases the problem is less complex : the representative of the funding organisation is too much a product of his or her own society, culture and way of thinking to have open eyes and ears for his or her counterparts from the South. Moreover, many of them derive power and prestige from their position.

Challenges for the future

In view of the problems which are faced at present by the private development cooperation sector in the North, a searching debate about the future of (private) development cooperation seems to be desirable. The organisations have an obligation in this respect, not only to themselves but even more to the poor and oppressed in the South, people whose causes they claim to champion. A fundamental repositioning seems not to be illogical. After the spectacular growth and popularity of the 1970s and 1980s an atmosphere of complacency took hold, while both internally and in society at large, more and more doubts arose as to the benefits of aid[15]. In such a reflection process, four factors might be analysed in depth.

Several authors have argued that the dominant paradigm of 'development', as a direct continuation of 500 years of colonial history, is rooted in a deep belief in the superiority of Western people, their knowledge and technology and of Western civilisation as a whole (Sachs (ed.), 1992; Schrijvers, 1993; Shiva 1988, 1993). This approach is closely related to a number of characteristics in European thought such as control of the environment, the belief that change leads to progress, reductionism; a fragmented approach, a linear perception of time, and the fact that the idea 'that there is a limit to everything' has been obscured (Sizoo, 1993; Shiva, 1988). From the South, from all three continents, there has been a growing opposition in recent years to this dominance (see among others Shiva, 1988, 1993). On the conceptual as well as on the normative levels, and on the level of practical implementation, the dominant paradigm needs to be challenged and changed.

At the conceptual level, development is not a linear process which moves in a single direction. The normative level is simple: 'Development should be people oriented, people come before things, and poor people come before the less poor' (Chambers, 1993: 1-14). At the empirical and implementation levels, development should be more 'from below and within' (Huizer, 1992).

In the second place, a serious reflection should take place regarding the aims, objectives and role of NGDOs in the North. The Third World no longer exists. This '...will require a radical rethinking of North-South relations since the traditional frameworks for understanding and explaining this relationship are no longer so convincing' (McGrew, 1992: 271). The question remains whether the financing of development activities should continue to be the most important objective. Should not the main issue be, as some people have been arguing for decades, to change international power relationships? (Achterhuis, 1973; Huizer, 1978). Political lobbying and development education might receive more systematic attention. Neo-liberal policy in combination with NGDOs as 'ladles in the global soup kitchen', is one step forward and two steps back (Fowler, 1994).

In the third place, a change in the (working) relationship between NGDOs in the North and South, beyond development cooperation, is urgent. The traditional relation of 'donor' and 'receiver' should be drastically changed. Staff of development organisations too easily take for granted Western value systems while themes such as 'aid and power' are insufficiently analysed (Sizoo, 1993). In the interaction between development organisations from the North and their counterpart organisations from the South, interaction, exchange, listening, open beginning and end, mutual interest and solidarity, and development as a learning process should become key words.

Finally, in the fourth place, within the current development cooperation system, improvement of quality should be made a higher priority. Effectiveness of development cooperation is probably more restricted than generally suggested. The effectiveness of programmes on the macro-economic level in particular leaves much to be desired (Rinnooy Kan, 1993). There is no reason whatsoever to believe that the situation with regard to private cooperation is much better. The situation is probably as described tersely by Graham Hancock: 'by and large, I believe their staff to be well motivated and their efforts worthwhile ... They rarely do significant harm; sometimes they do great good' (Hancock, 1991: xiii).

Attention to increased effectiveness should demand the highest priority. Not the intentions, but the results of development work should be central. This means that study and evaluation, and particularly feedback from real-life situations, should prevail.

It is still questionable, however, whether private organisations are able to perform such a cultural somersault. Smillie observes pithily: 'Northern non-governmental development organisations are in trouble' (Smillie & Helmich, 1993: 14). Over the next few years much will depend on the question, in how far private development organisations are willing to reconsider their premises, to reflect on their objectives, to give shape to a more evenly balanced relation with their colleagues in the South and to strive for quality improvement in many areas.

NOTES

1. This is not to say that the Soviet Union of that period and the countries in Eastern Europe were not inspired by political and economical motives in their relationships with former colonies. During the period 1945-1989, however, there were important differences both in the objectives and in implementation when compared with development aid from Western countries. See for example Nayyar (ed.), 1975.
2. Essential in Chomsky's argumentation is that the governments of the United States and Western Europe had protected their national production, not only in the industrial domain, but also in agriculture and fishery, from the beginning of the colonial period (i.e. for centuries).
3. This book confines itself to those non-governmental organisations which carry out 'development' activities. They may be called non-governmental development organisations (Shah, 1991: 6). Furthermore, a distinction can be made between primary and intermediate organisations. Primary organisations are from and on behalf of the poor; intermediate organisations work for the benefit of certain target groups or offer their services to other organisations (UNDP, 1993: 84-85).
4. This is actually an area which needs to be looked into in greater depth. It would be interestingly and important, to analyse to what extent, and in what way, the policies and activities at operational level of private development organisations deviate from the governmental assistance. In Chapter 3 of this book the results of the policies and activities of the Dutch government and the Dutch-based non-governmental development organisation ICCO are compared. See also Chapter 8 in which, among other things, the specific roles of the various actors in development are discussed.
5. The number of officially registered NGDOs in OECD countries increased from 1,600 in 1980 to 2,970 in 1993 (Smillie and Helmich, 1994). A similar growth has been observed in many countries in the South (for instance in Bolivia, Nepal, India and Tunesia).
6. The definition of participation in this context is somewhat mechanical (a means rather than a goal in itself).
7. Apart from this more or less mechanical view, participation can also be linked to tackling the structural causes of people's poverty, rather than as yet another

input to a development project (Oakley, 1994).

8. A number of these problems and dilemmas might also be applicable to bilateral and multilateral aid programmes. For instance, the official development assistance (ODA) is most probably not more effective, with difficulty – or not at all – reaches the 'poorest of the poor', is equally prone to impose Western value systems, and normally does not shy away from projecting a rather rosy picture of its activities. However, the present chapter confines itself to the private development cooperation sector.
9. This section is largely based on: South Commission (1990), UNDP (1991), the World Development Report (World Bank, 1990) as well as on later UNDP and World Bank publications. It should be noticed, however, that these reports are rather limited as they do not provide an historical analysis of developmental processes, do not differentiate between sections of the population and regions within countries, and do not pay attention to gender issues (Schrijvers, 1993).
10. In the early 1980s aid amounted to about nine per cent of the Gross National Product (GNP) in the 'least developed countries', and three per cent for other low-income countries. In countries with medium-sized income this was two per cent. For individual countries the figure varied from one to twenty per cent. For all poor countries, the development aid figure is momentarily well above one per cent of their GNP. Only the share of development assistance in the GNP of countries in sub-Saharan Africa has risen to more than ten per cent (UNDP,1990).
11. Moreover, it should be realised that the reverse flow of money is much larger. For instance, the special loan redemptions and interest payments in 1988 resulted in a net flow of 32.5 billion from South to North (UNDP Report, 1990).
12. It is for instance arguable that the termination of Dutch financing of private organisations in Indonesia in the period 1992-2000 has had negative effects for the NGDOs concerned and the NGDO sector in this country as such.
13. For an overview of recent literature about this subject see Chapter 2.
14. Alan Fowler, personal communication.
15. It is remarkable that within some of the multilateral institutions the need for 'a major reassssment of aid programmes' is acknowledged. The authors of the World Economic and Social Survey 1995 raised the question 'Official Development assistance (ODA): end of an era?, argue 'The point is that after two, three, or more decades, the model whereby the North "assists" the South to develop through ODA programmes and projects – including those of the multilateral institutions – has to be re-examined', and put forward some ideas about 'a new model of development cooperation' (United Nations, 1995: 130 & 138- 139).

when to a development project (Oakley [illegible]).

8. A number of these problems and dilemmas might also be applicable to bilateral and multilateral aid programmes. For instance, the official development assistance (ODA) is most probably not more effective, with difficulty – or not at all – reaches the 'poorest of the poor', is equally prone to impose Western value systems, and normally does not shy away from projecting a rather rosy picture of its activities. However, the present chapter confines itself to the private development cooperation sector.

9. This section is largely based on: South Commission (1990); UNDP (1991); the World Development Report (World Bank, 1990) as well as on later UNDP and World Bank publications. It should be noticed, however, that these reports are rather limited as they do not provide an historical analysis of developmental processes, do not differentiate between sections of the population and regions within countries, and do not pay attention to gender issues (Schrijvers, 1993).

10. In the early 1980s aid amounted to about nine per cent of the Gross National Product (GNP) in the least developed countries, and three per cent for other low-income countries. In countries with medium-sized income, this was two per cent. For individual countries the figure varied from one to twenty per cent. For all poor countries, the development aid figure is, momentarily, well above one per cent of their GNP. Only the share of development assistance in the GNP of countries in sub-Saharan Africa has risen to more than ten per cent (UNDP, 1990).

11. Moreover, it should be realised that the reverse flow of money is much larger. For instance, the special loan redemption and interest payments in 1988 resulted in a net flow of \$32.5 billion from South to North (UNDP Report, 1990).

12. It is for instance arguable that the termination of Dutch co-financing of private organisations in Indonesia in the period 1992–1996 has had negative effects for the NGDOs concerned and the NGDO sector in that country as a whole.

13. For an overview of recent literature about this subject see Chapter 2.

14. Alan Fowler, personal communication.

15. It is remarkable that within some of the multilateral institutions the need for a major reassessment of aid programmes is acknowledged. The authors of the World Economic and Social Survey 1995 raised the question 'Official Development assistance (ODA): end of an era?' arguing 'The pattern of the last two, three, or more decades, the model whereby the North "assists" the South to develop through ODA programmes and projects – including those of the multilateral institutions – has to be re-examined' and further, and something about 'a new model of development cooperation' (United Nations, 1995: 133 & 135–139).

PART - II

EFFECTIVENESS OF NGDOS

2

THE FUNCTIONING OF NON-GOVERNMENTAL DEVELOPMENT ORGANISATIONS IN INDIA

— *Lau Schulpen* and *Fons van der Velden*

Since the 1980s non-governmental development organisations (NGDOs) have been attributed a special and unique role in the process of development of Third World countries. Only in recent years the effectiveness, efficiency and relevance for development of both Southern and Northern (donor) NGDOs have been subject to more in-depth investigation. This chapter examines the functioning and policies of ICCO, a Dutch donor NGDO. Preceded by an overview of ICCO's policy with reference to India and the nature and magnitude of the projects that were approved for financing between 1971-1993, an assessment is made of the relevance, efficiency and effectiveness of the counterpart organisations over a period of time (1971-1988). The chapter ends with more recent policy developments resulting from the assessment.

The role of NGDOs

In the 1990s, international organisations such as the World Bank and the IMF as well as the Indian government have emphasised that non-governmental development organisations (NGDOs) can play an important role in the implementation of poverty alleviation programmes in India. In January 1992, while presenting the National Bravery Awards to children, the then Prime Minister, Mr. P.V.

Narasimha Rao, even said: 'I am prepared to hand over the villages, blocks and zones to the voluntary organisations and non-governmental agencies'.

Not surprisingly, NGDOs themselves are their own most dedicated supporters. Many NGDOs (in South and North), driven by their great optimism about the relevance, efficiency and effectiveness of their work, present themselves as ideal channels for aid and as having a positive impact in such fields as poverty reduction and democratisation. In general, it is argued that (donor) NGDOs have specific comparative advantages over other players in the development field. These advantages not only refer to their dedicated, value-driven and self-motivated staff and their closeness to the poor, but also to their innovative approaches, flexibility and ability to perform different tasks (Fowler & Biekart, 1996: 107-112). It often was (and still is) stated that NGDOs are effective organisations because they are closer to the target group, supposedly better at reaching the very poorest, 'ideal vehicles and agents for participatory development and key actors in strategies to empower the poor and excluded', and also because they are highly valued 'as instruments to reduce state intervention and promote the privatization of development action' (Stiefel & Wolfe, 1994: 206). In short, NGDOs seek two common types of results and also claim that they contribute to these: 'alleviation of poverty and strengthening civil society through enhancing participation of grassroots organisations'. Added then is, however, that 'making claims [...] is one thing, backing them up with evidence is another story altogether'. Assessing the performance of NGDOs – whether in the field of poverty alleviation, democratisation, building civil society, or leadership training – is extremely difficult. Fowler (1997: 160) has remarked that 'when it comes to knowing the results of their efforts, NGOs rate poorly'. It should be stressed that this holds not only for Southern NGDOs but for Northern (donor) NGDOs as well.

Overview of ICCO's India policy

Within the framework of the Dutch Co-financing Programme (see Chapter 3) the Interchurch Organisation for Development Cooperation (ICCO), since its inception in 1964, finances private development organisations in Third World countries. Approximately 100 persons are employed at its office in the Netherlands. In 1999 ICCO made available about NLG 205 million to some 70 countries in the Third World. Together with Cordaid (Catholic) and Novib (secular), ICCO (Protestant) is one of the largest private development organisations in the Netherlands.

ICCO's involvement in development activities in India has greatly increased during the period under review here in terms of the amount of money that has been made available for organisations in India, the number of projects financed and staff of the India project unit. For our purpose, a distinction is made between the following periods.

The period 1964-1975

In accordance with ICCO's identity, contacts were established mainly with Protestant-Christian (development) organisations, such as the Young Men Christian Association, the Young Women Christian Association, the Salvation Army, and several Protestant churches. From the early 1970s onwards the Dutch government approved ICCO projects in the area of healthcare and (vocational) education in India. In line with the then prevailing development conceptions, many of these projects focused on the transfer of knowledge. As agreed upon between the Dutch government and the co-financing organisations (MFOS) they did not include current expenditures; the support was related to buildings or the purchase of equipment.

The period 1976-1985

In the early 1970s the Co-financing Programme underwent several major policy, procedural and financial changes, including the adoption of a target group policy; current expenditures were allowed as part of a project; for the approval of a project the assent of the government of a developing country was no longer required; and a fixed percentage (4.8 per cent) of the Dutch budget for development cooperation was to be allocated to the Co-financing Programme.

In 1974 and 1975 ICCO staff and board had already started discussions on the question to what extent ICCO should become more systematically involved in the support of development organisations in India. Taking into account a variety of factors (increased funds for co-financing, the new target group policy, and the magnitude of the poverty problem in India), the ICCO board decided to move towards concentrated attention for India. A special India desk was established in 1976.

In 1975, it had also been decided that in India ICCO would no longer confine itself to the support of organisations of Protestant-Christian origin. This policy change became noticeable in 1976 when, for the first time, a project of a secular organisation (AWARE, Hyderabad) was approved. At the same time ICCO continued to pursue an active policy towards Protestant-Christian organisations, its 'historical partners'. During the period 1976-1980 the contacts with these organisations (including the National Council of Churches) were extended, also in depth. A network of consultants (individuals and institutions) was built up and the first contacts were made with secular organisations, among which non-institutionalised organisations or social action groups.

The new target group policy meant an emphasis on the support to particular dalits (untouchables), tribal and/or marginal and landless people. In the assessment of project applications more attention than before was paid to the analysis of the target groups and their participation in the implementation of the programmes. In rural areas the focus was on community development projects; in urban areas priority was given to projects in slums.

The policy to finance only fixed assets in India (buildings, machinery) was left in 1976 when ICCO started to co-finance programme expenditure as well. Until the same year the two major categories for support were education and healthcare. From that year on, however, community development (with agriculture and healthcare as main components) became predominant.

Several factors contributed to these changes. Firstly, the discussions held in 1976 between the Dutch government and the MFOs resulted in greater responsibility of the MFOs for the financial and technical project procedures. The possibilities for MFOs to make independent decisions regarding projects to be supported were further enlarged in 1980 when the MFOs were given an annual block grant with accountability afterwards for the entire amount of money (see Chapter 3). Secondly, in 1978 ICCO launched its overall policy plan Development and Participation in which the participation in developmental processes of the people concerned was laid down. The changes in ICCO's policy were also inspired by the type of requests for the financing of projects it received, the experiences it had gained in the practice of project financing and new scientific opinions with regard to processes of change in developing countries (see, for instance, Oman & Wignaraja, 1991; Hettne, 1990).

In the early 1980s the policies, that had been developed in 1975, 1976 regarding the support of development projects, were further elaborated and put into practice in an increasing number of approved projects. In 1983, the capacity of the India desk was enlarged. The number of projects increased, including a growing number of follow-up projects. Participation of the target group and efforts towards structural change became ever more important criteria in the assessment of new applications and the number of projects of non-Christian and non-institutionalised organisations (including action groups) increased as well.

The period 1986-1992

In this period of reflection, growing attention to policy design, further fine-tuning of priorities and more objective criteria were developed to enhance the assessment of project proposals. An internal evaluation of all projects and organisations, that had been supported between 1971 and 1988 (see the section on assessment of quality projects below), induced a process which resulted, among other things, in the formulation of the new assessment criteria at the end of the 1980s.

After his visit to six ICCO-supported large rural development organisations (the so-called BINGOs or Big NGOs) in India in 1986, the director of ICCO presented a proposal with far-reaching policy implications. The proposal, aimed at further expansion of ICCO's involvement in India, promoted more extensive support to BINGOs. The ICCO management explained this by stating: 1) there seems to be a reasonable good participation of the target group in the projects at the village level; 2) the Indian government seems at the moment to provide sufficient room for this type of activity; 3) the leaders of the national NGOs seem to possess sufficient pragmatism and realism not to go beyond what is (politically) acceptable; 4) in a large number of villages, economic development is clearly visible; 5) these programmes reach the people who belong to the poorest in the world; 6) although the project sums are large, the investments per capita are limited; and 7) the mentioned organisations seem to have sufficient and qualified staff. In conclusion, the large-scale rural development activities for five of the six NGDOs can 'be seen as a positive contribution to the creation of facilities for development of the poor rural population based on self-help' (ICCO, 1986).[1]

This proposal would have major consequences for the India desk: growth of the budget for India from NLG 13 to 20 million, institutionalising of programme and organisation financing, and staff increases. More concentrated attention for BINGOs did not occur,[2] however, and the 20 million budget for India was never reached. The proposal did have consequences for the decision-making process and the organisation of the desk. Programme and organisation funding became an accepted form of financing.[3] The discussions on the expansion of the India desk were a first step towards the integration of the preparation and monitoring staff which took shape as the so-called 'India experiment II' in 1987 (ICCO, 1988).[4] In other papers specific topics relating to policy development were touched upon. In a short introductory paper concerning ICCO's involvement in India the concept of empowerment was introduced (ICCO, 1987a).[5] The paper also paid attention to the BINGO discussion and confirmed the need for further strengthening of 'support and consultancy organisations'.[6]

In the late 1980s and the early1990s ICCO organised internal staff consultations to discuss policy development and improvement of the quality of its activities in general. For the 1990 consultation the India desk prepared a policy paper (ICCO, 1990) based on the preliminary results of an internal evaluation of the activities supported in India during the period 1971-1988. The discussions led to several new policy recommendations. It was suggested to drastically reduce the number of projects in order to come to a more manageable package of projects.[7] A switch in regional priorities was also suggested. The most interesting recommendation in this context was the establishment of a special group comprising those states in which the majority of the supported projects were located. A very selective policy would be pursued with regard to applications from this group.

The prospect of more intensive and long-lasting relations with ecumenical counterparts was also held out while income-generating projects were given the highest priority. For the first time specific attention was given to women. The desk held to its 'two-track policy', i.e. attention to projects targeting women and attention to integrated projects with women as a component. The integrated approach should also apply to health projects (i.e. health as part of a socio-economic and political programme). In contrast to previous policies, it was proposed to pay more attention to projects aimed at the urban poor, and to pose restrictions on the availability of funds. 'Recent analyses have taught that in the past a number of NGOs supported by ICCO have grown too fast and have been overfinanced. The desk therefore proposes to continue the policy of tight financing; to insist on a substantial own contribution [...] and to indicate in a growing number of cases the finiteness of the ICCO support, so that from 1992 onwards a minimum of 20 per cent of the allocation [for India] is available for new, innovating projects' (ICCO, 1990:7).[8]

It was also suggested to maintain the allocation for India at the same level (40 per cent of the Asia budget). By reducing the number of projects/counterparts room would be created for the financing of bigger projects and/or bigger NGDOs. Part of the funds should also be made available to support organisations active at a national level. Relations with existing support organisations should be intensified, while an expansion was envisaged in the areas of ecology, women and development, and income-generating activities. The policy paper also stressed the need for a change in project assessment and monitoring, in particular concerning the bigger projects and counterparts. This suggests that nothing much had happened in this area since the BINGO discussion in 1986. Although some of the points mentioned in the 1990 policy paper were to be further elaborated in the years to follow,[9] the lines set out in the paper were fairly fixed. The formal 1993 Policy Profile (which will be discussed in more detail in the section on recent policy developments) can therefore be seen as mainly a public confirmation and to some extent further refinement of the 1990 paper.

Project financing[10]

The above outline of ICCO's India policy between 1971 and 1993 was realised through the funding of 958 projects.[11] During the period 1971-1975 the total number of projects, that were approved for financing, was 15. After 1976 the number of approved projects grew each year, especially during the 1980s. The early 1990s, however, show a strong decline (see Table 2.1).

Over nine per cent (89 projects) were so-called 'All-India'

projects: projects carried out by organisations active throughout India. The remaining 869 projects were implemented in one or more states in India, with some states well ahead. More than half of the projects were located in three states: Andhra Pradesh, West Bengal and Tamil Nadu.[12] There was a concentration of projects in Southern states, Maharashtra and West Bengal, while the Northern states Haryana, Punjab and Himachal Pradesh were appreciably underrepresented.

Table 2.1 : General (financial) data regarding the projects approved by ICCO in India (x million Dutch guilders)

Year	Number of projects	Total cost of projects	ICCO commitment	SP contribution	Own contribution	Other resources
1971-1975	15	14.0	6.0	—	2.1	5.9
1976-1980	125	47.3	31.8	0.8	9.7	5.0
1981-1985	258	88.0	48.6	3.8	13.3	22.3
1986-1990	392	180.9	64.0	15.3	47.2	54.4
1991-1993	168	112.2	40.7	6.6	15.1	49.8
Total	958	442.4	191.1	26.5	87.4	137.4

Source : Authors' calculation based on data from ICCO's administration

Notes : The 'ICCO commitment' represents the total amount ICCO set aside in the year concerned for projects in India. Hence, this does not refer to the actual expenditure per year.
The SP contribution represents a contribution from additional funds from the Dutch government (DGIS) or the European Community.

In the period 1971-1993 the total ICCO contribution to the 958 projects amounted to more than NLG 191 million (see table 2.1), with an average contribution of nearly NLG 200,000 per project. Between 1971 and 1990 the average contribution decreased considerably; only the three very first projects ICCO financed, which were large hospital projects (so-called brick and mortar projects), each received about NLG 500,000. In the 1980s the average contribution exceeded NLG 200,000 only once, resulting from the policy swift towards the financing of community development projects. The declining number of counterparts and the increasing focus on organisation and programme financing (instead of projects) led to a significant growth of the average contribution in the early 1990s: over NLG 200,000 in 1991, less than NLG 190,000 in 1992 and even over NLG 300,000 in 1993.

In addition to the ICCO contribution there is often a contribution from special funds (the Dutch government or the European Community), from other donors and/or from the aid recipient itself (see table 2.1).[13] In spite of the relatively substantial increase in the total cost of the projects as from the mid-1980s, ICCO's contribution to these cost decreased until the early 1990s. The contributions from the special funds (SP) of the Dutch Government and the European Community, which started in 1978, were rather limited during the first years, cut off in 1981 and 1982, and raised considerably in 1987. As from 1988 the contribution from this source to ICCO projects in India fluctuates between NLG 1.5 and 2 million per year. In 1991, however, the SP contribution suddenly doubled and in 1993 there was no such contribution at all.[14]

Both the total costs of the projects supported by ICCO and the contributions from various sources reached their highest point in 1987, 1988 and 1991. The volume of new commitments decreased substantially from 1989 onwards, in India (see table 2.1) as well as in general. In 1988 the expenditure capacity came under pressure due to a smaller increase of ICCO resources than was expected, and the accumulation of high financial obligations from long-term agreements. The ICCO management then took steps to reduce the share of previous financial commitments to create (and maintain) sufficient financial space for policy renewal.[15]

Type of projects

Between 1971-1975 construction projects represented almost 87 per cent of the total number of approved projects. This percentage dropped to two in the period 1985-1990 and to nil over 1991-1993 (see table 2.2). Similar to developments in many other donor agencies, there was a noticeable shift from infrastructural to so-called community development projects in ICCO as well. During the 1980s, the latter represented the major part of the project range. The number of healthcare projects also increased in the period 1976-1980; during the period 1971-1993 fourteen per cent of the projects were in this sector. In the same period, projects in the sectors human rights, legal aid and refugees were approved only incidentally. Finally, the rise in the number of emergency aid projects in the second half of the 1980s is noteworthy but temporary.[16]

Up to the beginning of the 1980s new projects, both in terms of number and ICCO contribution, remained more important than follow-up projects. In the course of the decade this picture changed fundamentally. Whereas in 1987 twenty-eight of the 81 approved

Table 2.2 : ICCO projects per sector (in percentage of total)

	1971-1975	1976-1980	1981-1985	1986-1990	1991-1993	Total
Community development		22	38	46	39	39
Healthcare	7	16	13	12	18	14
Construction healthcare	47	16	5	1		5
Education and training		6	11	9	10	9
Construction training	40	7	5	1		4
Agriculture and land development	7	8	1	3	5	4
Economic & industrial activity		7	4	2	2	3
General activities		6	9	10	10	9
Habitat, infrastructure		9	4	2	1	4
Communication/media			6	3	1	3
Emergency aid		2	1	6	1	3
Human rights				1	1	0
Legal assistance			2	1		1
Refugees				0		0
Organisation building					2	0
Primary productive sector					5	1
Community work					5	1
Total (in absolute figures)	15	125	258	392	168	958

Source : Authors' calculation based on data from ICCO's administration

Note : From 1993 onwards, community development is no longer a specific sector and new sectors have been introduced.

projects can be characterised as 'new', this only applies to five out of the 72 projects approved in 1991. The allocation of ICCO funds to new projects dropped from more than 35 per cent in 1981 to 3.7 per cent in 1990. As a consequence, the room for engaging into new relationships with new counterpart organisations and the initiation of innovative projects with 'old' counterparts was very limited.[17] It also indicates that the number of ICCO counterparts in India had remained fairly stable over the period under review. It can therefore be stated that ICCO practised programme financing through the financing of projects.[18]

Target groups

In ICCO's internal registration the target group of more than half of the projects in the period 1971-1990 is described as 'poor people'. For the other half about twenty different designators are mentioned in the documents, from rag pickers to tenants and from hospital staff to leather workers. Whatever the designator may be, it is evident that the majority of the target groups of ICCO's counterpart organisations in India belong to the lower strata of society. The same appears from their cultural identity: the target groups of 42 per cent of the projects are tribal populations, harijans (dalits) and/ or lower castes.

Nearly 68 per cent of all projects target people in rural areas, about nine per cent people in urban areas and the remainder people in both rural and urban areas. In the last 20 years little has changed in this respect.

Finally, when looking at sex division, it is noteworthy in the first place that in two-thirds of the projects there is no indication whether they target men, women, or men and women. Until 1987 there was an increase in projects specifically targeting women (from one in 1971 to six in 1987), than dropping to one in 1990. The percentile share of projects targeting women was therefore relatively low (5.9 per cent in the period 1971-1990). The most significant increase was in projects with women as a component: from one in 1977 to 31 in 1990 (in the latter year thus 43 per cent of all projects).

Counterparts

As mentioned before ICCO has actually practised a form of programme financing in India. A large number of organisations have received financial support for a long period of time and for a great variety of projects. AWARE in Andhra Pradesh is a case in point. It has been supported from as early as 1976 and, until the end of 1993, 39 projects were approved in sectors varying from emergency aid to community development projects.

The 958 projects, that were financed in the period 1971-1993 were implemented by 281 different organisations.[19] Although data on the background of these NGDOs is only available upto 1992, it is clear that from 1971 onwards the diversity in background of ICCO's counterparts in India has increased considerably. The majority of the organisations (64 per cent of the total number), are of Protestant-Christian origin or have (close) ties to the Protestant-Christian community and/or Church in India (see table 2.3), while 27 per cent are registered as secular organisations. The remaining organisations either have a Gandhian background or have connections with Hindu or Muslim communities.

Table 2.3 : ICCO contribution per identity organisation 1971-1990 (in percentage)

Identity	1971-75	1976-80	1981-85	1986-90	1991-92	Total
Christian	100	66	40	18	26	37
Christian secular		12	33	32	29	27
Secular		19	17	39	31	27
Gandhian		1	9	10	13	8
Hindu/Muslim		2	2			1
Total	100	100	100	100	100	100

Initially (1971-1975) only Christian organisations were supported. During 1976-1980 they received 66 per cent of the ICCO funds and secular organisations 19 per cent. Between 1986 and

1990 the secular organisations received more than NLG 25 million (39 per cent). Consequently, Christian and secular organisations together accounted for 50 per cent. For the entire period the Christian organisations, both in terms of number and of ICCO contribution, were the most important, followed by the secular and Christian-secular organisations.[20] Gandhian organisations and those with a Hindu or Muslim background made up nine per cent of the number of organisations, accounting for eight per cent of the ICCO contribution during 1971-1990.

Assessment of quality projects

Until the present no, or hardly any, general studies have been made into the relevance for development, efficiency and effectiveness of the ICCO-supported private development organisations in India. Apart from the so-called programme evaluations and the Dutch Impact Study, studies and assessments were virtually only conducted into single projects or organisations.[21] Project reports provide insufficient insight into the quality of the work supported by ICCO in India at large.

In 1989 internal assessments were made of the activities of all 257 organisations that ICCO had supported between 1971-1988. The assessments were carried out by individual staff members of the India desk on the basis of, among other things, progress reports, (field) visits to counterparts, and internal and external evaluation reports. The organisations were classified on a one to five assessment scale. The individual assessments were subsequently discussed by the entire desk staff, sometimes resulting in changes being made.

The assessments were made on the basis of four criteria: a) the relevance of the organisation in the context of the socio-economic and political situation of the target group in the operational region; b) efficiency; c) the effectivity of the programme; and d) accountability of the implementing organisation to the target group, constituent elements, within the own organisation and to the funding organisation (i.e. ICCO). The latter, somewhat anomalous, criterion was added as in the Co-financing Programme, it is supposed that non-governmental development organisations can and do reach the poor effectively through their direct contacts. Besides, the accountability mechanisms of NGDOs – particularly in respect of the poor – usually are a critical area.

In spite of the fact that the activities of the 257 organisations were not in all cases assessed systematically, and that the assessment to some extent could be characterised as a subjective post-evaluation, the results present an indicative picture regarding the relevance, efficiency and effectiveness of the activities of ICCO's counterparts in India.

The quality of the activities of 39 per cent of the organisations was assessed as positive to very positive, while the impact of the work of 21 per cent of the organisations was found to be insufficient (see table 2.4). For the remaining 40 per cent of the organisations a definite conclusion could not be reached for a variety of reasons. The latter organisations had carried out the projects more or less as agreed, but there were doubts about the sustainability of the activities.

Table 2.4 : Assessment categories: number of organisations, ICCO contribution and number of projects (period 1971-1988)

	Number of organisations (in %)	ICCO contribution (in %)	Number of projects
(Very) negative	21	11	109
Unclear	40	30	227
(Very) positive	39	60	309
Total	100	100	645

The organisations which were negatively assessed by the ICCO staff, both with regard to the implementation and the impact of the projects, received 11 per cent of the total ICCO contribution to projects in India during the entire period 1971-1988. The majority of these organisations (nearly 63 per cent) had been supported to an amount less than NLG 250,000. The positively judged organisations had received approximately 60 per cent of the total ICCO contribution. Most of the organisations in this group had received a large amount of money as a contribution to the project cost: 26 organisations each more than NLG one million. The organisations about which a clear assessment could not be given, accounted for 30 per cent of the total ICCO contribution. The majority of them had not received more than NLG 250,000; 11 organisations received more than NLG one million.

Next to the organisations, the staff of ICCO's India desk also assessed the separate projects in 1989, using the same method. Forty-eight per cent of the 645 projects in the period 1971-1988 received a positive to very positive classification. Of a large number – more than 35 per cent – a clear picture could not be formed, while the remaining 17 per cent performed unsatisfactory. Projects with a high ICCO contribution were more frequently assessed positively than projects which had received a low contribution. Of the projects with an ICCO contribution up to NLG 250,000, 44 per cent were found to be positive. This percentage increases to 59.5 per cent for projects to which ICCO contributed more than NLG two million. Hardly any project financed by additional funds from the Dutch Ministry for Development Cooperation and/or the regular funds of the European Community were assed negatively.[22]

Sector-wise, there were some striking differences. For instance, half of all projects focusing on income generation were negatively assessed and only eight per cent positively. For the community development projects it was the other way around: 16 per cent received a negative and 54 per cent a positive judgement. In the sectors emergency aid, construction, education and training, and healthcare, the activities of more than half of the projects were considered satisfactory.

Problems at the side of the counterparts

The above data reveal a relevant ICCO investment in approximately 50 per cent of cases, while for the other half the effect is (still) unclear or nil. The effectiveness of the Co-financing Programme is connected to a set of problems at the side of the main actors: the implementing private development organisation in a Third World country and the funding agency in the West, in this case ICCO. With regard to the counterparts the following problems can be defined :

1. *Objectives* : Many organisations run into problems due to an inadequate analysis of the situation of the target group. Besides, in principle relevant objectives are often not effectively made operational in terms of measurable long and short-term objectives and activities. Hence, it may happen that an initially innovative rural healthcare project founders completely because, for instance, the changing position of the poor due to rapid urbanisation in the region has not been taken into consideration. On the other hand, a Gandhian organisation that has, in line with Chambers, Saxena & Shah (1989: 11-15) managed to translate the priorities of the poor Survival, Security and Self-respect very clearly, is exceptionally efficient and effective.
2. *Project implementation* : Organisations that score low often perform poorly with regard to planning, monitoring and evaluation of activities. There are only a few organisations with a properly functioning internal reporting system to determine the progress of the project. Negatively assessed organisations rarely carry out (self-)evaluations.
3. *Materials* : More successful organisations, including several Gandhian ones, only use materials appropriate to the local context and/or culture which, consequently, do not have an alienating effect. In weaker organisations such alienating elements are quite often encountered.
4. *Staff* : Organisations, that score low, in many cases employ unqualified and/or inexperienced staff. In integrated projects the 'technicians' often cannot communicate with the 'social workers' and vice versa. Many social workers supervise economic projects without being properly trained. It is also noteworthy that a number of staff members in the NGDO sector

have managed to acquire a higher social position than would have been possible in the commercial or public sectors. It should be noted that salaries in the NGDO sector in India are generally exceptionally low; virtually everyone has an appointment 'on the condition of financing being available'. However, surveys also show that the indirect benefits (free housing, medical facilities, transport, telephone and subsidised food) are generally high (Patni, 1990). According to the researchers, in Gandhian organisations approximately 12-18 per cent of the total expenditure is used for the remuneration of staff. For organisations run by professionals this percentage is 30-40 and for Christian organisations 35-40. A large number of successful organisations have honest, capable project directors, while the management of several other organisations lack the education, skill and experience to provide adequate leadership and direction to the organisation.

5. *Financial management* : In contrast to negatively assessed organisations, much attention is paid to financial policy and management in (very) positively assessed organisations.[23]
6. *Organisational strength* : Many of the unsuccessful projects are run by organisationally weak executives. There are no clear-cut authorities and responsibilities, internal control and accountability mechanisms are lacking, and the accountability towards the target group, management and funding organisations leaves much to be desired.

In conclusion, it can be stated that relatively inefficient and ineffective organisations are often conceptually weak. They have difficulty in formulating objectives and operational plans. The quality of the project implementation, financial policy and management is poor, and the staff is often insufficiently equipped for their task. Moreover, the organisation itself is often not properly organised.[24]

ICCO's role

The limited effectiveness of ICCO's co-financing programme in

India cannot be attributed only to the counterparts. ICCO's policy and project management play a part as well. In the first place, it appears that in the processing of funding applications projects were assessed in a rather isolated way. Factors at the meso or macro level and the relevance for development, in particular the significance of the proposed intervention for the poor, were sometimes poorly considered.

In the second place, the project implementation capacity of applying organisations was insufficiently analysed. In the project screening process such aspects as internal organisation, orientation and reputation of the organisation, and their project planning, monitoring and evaluation capacity received too little attention.

In the third place, the assessment mainly focused on proposed activities, i.e. the planning stages, while relatively little attention was paid to the quality and the relevance for the poor of the activities that had already been carried out.

A fourth factor which influenced the quality of ICCO's project processing was the so-called budgetary pressure as a consequence of, among other things, the increase in the total amount of money available for funding for ICCO as a whole and the India desk in particular. The growth of funds induced the rapid approval of new and follow-up projects as well as a fast expansion of the programme of several NGDOs. Sometimes new projects were approved with no visit beforehand by ICCO staff, consultants or advisers.[25]

Finally, separate mention should be made of the problems relating to the so-called EC block grant projects. For many years, the India desk used EC funds to finance the operating costs of new counterparts. Because these project applications could be approved simply and quickly, projects were included in ICCO's India programme which, despite the lack of information and/or poor quality of the work delivered, became regular ICCO projects through follow-up financing.

Lessons learnt

Several researchers have pointed out that attention for the quality of projects of co-financing is of great importance (for instance Quarles van Ufford, Kruijt & Downing, 1988; Quarles van Ufford & Wils, 1991). Quarles van Ufford states that in the early years of the Co-financing Programme control of quality was mainly related to 'the accountability for the money to be spent' and later to 'problems of regulation and controllability... The balance between the organisational means and the objectives had to be restored' (Quarles van Ufford & Wils, 1991: 29-57). In his opinion the latter received special attention during the period 1978-1988. In the late 1980s, a period he characterises as one of 'isolation' and 'growth', the focus should be on control of the quality, especially the content, of implemented projects and programmes, i.e. of the activities and policy carried out.

Since the early 1990s ICCO has taken several interrelated measures to solve the problems with regard to the processing of project applications. The measures (some on overall ICCO level, others region related) should improve the quality of ICCO's activities and the effectiveness of the activities of ICCO-supported organisations. Within ICCO more systematic attention has been paid to policy formulation and testing. The former more project-oriented processing of projects – with emphasis on internal factors directly related to the funding proposal – was often inadequately connected to ICCO's overall policy guidelines (which, however, were hardly made operational) as laid down in the policy document Justice and Mercy. To redress this shortcoming general policy documents have been translated into regional (Asia, Latin America and Africa) and so-called sub-regional (for example India) country policy profiles, which have become the basis for project policy. Furthermore, evaluation of the policies and projects has received more attention with the establishment of the Evaluation and Policy desk in 1989.

Action has been taken to adjust the instruments that are used in the processing of new funding applications and in the monitoring of projects during implementation. The accent will then shift from an analysis of the planning process to an assessment of the effects in the implementation phase,[26] an assessment of the project implementation capacity of the applying organisation, and the relevance of the proposed activities in the light of the local and broader context.

At the regional (India) level, file studies, self-evaluations and external evaluations are used to systematically analyse the efficiency and effectiveness of the supported organisations and projects. Since 1989, this has resulted in the termination of the funding relationship with an appreciable number of counterparts. In order to be able to guarantee high quality project processing with unchanged staffing and turnover, it has also been decided to reduce the number of contacts with private development organisations, thus creating a controllable and qualitatively acceptable project programme.[27] More than in the past Indian consultancy organisations will be called in for the assessment of new funding applications in particular. These so-called pre-financing assessments often relate to the objectives and the proposed activities in view of the problems with which the poor in the region are faced; the project implementation capacity of the applying organisation; and of the impact of the projects and programmes completed so far.

Finally, it was decided to carry out (in many instances independent) surveys into the activities of ICCO-supported organisations. Accountability not only applies to ICCO counterparts, but also to ICCO itself.

Box 1 : Overview of policy priorities in the 1993-1995 Policy Profile

General policy priorities and starting point

- **ICCO's financial allocation to India should remain high (approximately 33 per cent of the total Asian allocation or NLG 14-15 million annually).**

- Further defining and strengthening of the non-funding role of ICCO by promoting capacity building and linking counterpart organisations with relevant support organisations.
- Priority is given to organisations which adopt an empowerment approach.
- A two-tier gender policy will be followed: 1) an active acquisition with regard to (small) women's organisations, and 2) attention to women and gender aspects in mixed organisations in an integrated way. Besides, priority will be given to support organisations with (the willingness to adopt) an integrated gender approach.
- Priority to projects with a positive impact on the environment and expansion of contacts with organisations active in the environmental field.
- Within an active policy towards Christian counterparts, priority is given to project applications from Church communities and dioceses and to projects 'which promote greater harmony, understanding and dialogue between people of different communities, faiths and ethnic groups'.
- ICCO will develop an active phasing out strategy and give preference to activities for which a substantial part is financed locally. These 'project implementation priorities' also include more attention to evaluation, organisational capacity to implement activities, and moving away from organisations with heavy overheads.
- The number of counterparts will be further reduced from approximately 170 in 1992 to 130 at the end of 1995.

Project financing priorities

- Intensification of support to regional and national support organisations.
- Continuation of support to small and large organisations.
- Priority for small and large organisations working in one (functionally) defined area.
- Special attention for urban poor as target group.
- Priority to landless and marginal peasants in rural areas and migrants, urban nomads and squatters in urban areas.
- Within target groups comprising of Scheduled Castes and Tribes, priority to programmes which specifically and systematically have children and women as a target group.
- A regional policy will be followed with 1) no projects acceptable for Goa, Harijana, Himachal Pradesh, Jammu and Kashmir, Kerala and the Punjab; 2) selective acceptance of projects in Andhra Pradesh, Gujarat, Karnataka, Maharashtra, Orissa, Tamil Nadu and West Bengal (plus in these states only acceptance of projects of new counterparts which have a high thematic priority); and 3) priority for projects in Bihar, Madhya Pradesh, North-east India, Rajasthan and Uttar Pradesh.
- In addition to projects related to women and to projects of an ecumenical background, priority for two themes/sectors: 1) access to means of production and projects which generate income, and 2) sustainable agriculture and environmental care.

- Within healthcare activities, priority for organisations opting for an integrated approach (i.e. as part of a social, economic and political programme).
- Priority to activities related to AIDS in a structural way and to the rehabilitation of disabled people.
- Within education: priority to 1) informal education as part of integrated projects; 2) vocational training projects with at least an equal number of women participates; and 3) (additional) training activities which promote access to the regular education system.
- Human rights activities and media projects are only accepted as part of an integrated project.
- Applications for emergency aid are only accepted from existing counterparts for projects in their own operational area. Besides, attention should also be geared at rehabilitation and emergency activities have to be linked to the regular programme of the organisation.

Source : ICCO, 1993b: 8-18.

Recent policy developments

In April 1993, ICCO presented its Policy Profile India for the period 1993-1995 (later extended to 1997 because of 'delays in the implementation of the policy and internal limitations' (ICCO, 1998:3)). Based on the conclusions of the above-described internal evaluation, a whole range of priorities have been established at general policy level as well as the project level. Box 1 not only provides an overview of these priorities, but also shows that the number of priorities is so high that there is a clear danger of over-prioritising. Central to the priorities is the integrated approach directed at empowerment. According to the Policy Profile (ICCO, 1993b: 9) empowerment 'attempts to meet the basic needs of the poor in a particular area by means of promoting literacy, education, organisation and mobilisation, vocational training, increasing incomes and resource management'. It is then concluded that empowerment thus 'means a sustainable development of the poor based on self-help'. The consequence of this integrated approach is that such different themes and sectors as human rights, healthcare, media and emergency aid can all be included in ICCO's India project portfolio, thus moving away from interventions focusing on only a (limited) part of the development problem.

Box 2 : Overview of policy priorities in the 1993-1997 Policy Profile

Allocation

- Policy: Stable at NLG 14-15 million annually.
- Outcome: Decline from NLG 13.8 million in 1991 to NLG 11.4 million in 1994 and subsequent increase to NLG 13.0 in 1997.

Number of partners

- Policy: Reduction from 170 in 1992 to 130 at the end of 1995.
- Outcome: Decline to about 100 counterparts in 1997 (and even further to some 90 in 1999).

Empowerment approach

- Policy: Priority to organisations following empowerment approach.
- Outcome: At least 50 per cent of counterparts work through an integrated programme of mobilisation bilisation, organisation, promoting literacy and education, healthcare, vocational training, increasing income and resource management. 25 per cent of the counterparts are focused on infrastructural and/or economic development (i.e., development approach) and the remaining 25 per cent are predominantly welfare oriented.

Gender

- Policy: Improving gender awareness and approach through gender training, a special gender-focused visit of a project officer, and gender dialogue with selected counterparts.
- Outcome: Workshops were held for staff of counterparts in 1996 and 1997 in cooperation with Brotfür die Welt, Christian Aid and EZE. 'These efforts contributed to further progress in gender sensitivity of desk officers and counterparts'. 'Further identification of critical factors and continued inputs are needed'.

Regional concentration

- Policy: Division in three areas (each consisting of different states) with 1) no priority; 2) selective acceptance and 3) priority.
- Outcome: Hardly realised - no full withdrawal from states like Kerala and only limited expansion in priority states like Madhya Pradesh, Uttar Pradesh and Rajasthan.

Source : ICCO, 1998: 6-9.

Note : Many priorities formulated in 1993 for the period upto 1995/1997 are not elaborated upon in the 1998 policy paper.

To what extent did ICCO manage to live up to its priorities? The Policy Profile India 1998-2002, presented in 1998,[28] should shed some light on this question as it is 'based on an internal review of the previous Policy Profile'. This review starts with the statement that the 'policy profile 1993-1995 was rather ambitious, with sometimes not sufficient operationalisation of the policy intentions and limited staff possibilities' (ICCO, 1998). Box 2 presents some major developments in the India programme of ICCO over the period 1993-1997 in relation to the policy priorities formulated for this period. Remarkably, ICCO equates an empowerment approach with an integrated programme. Some of the basic priorities formulated for the period 1993-1995/1997 have, as shown, been reached. This holds especially for the reduction in the number of counterparts. ICCO managed to go far beyond its policy by reducing this number by almost 50 per cent in seven years. Considering the relatively smaller decline in the annual budget for India, this means that the average ICCO contribution to its partners increased with one-third from NLG 154,000 in 1995 to NLG 201,000 in 1998. The 1998 Policy Paper states that regional concentration policy hardly materialised during 1993-1997. Nevertheless, calculations for the year 1998 show that ICCO certainly managed to reduce its disbursements in the (traditionally strongly represented) Southern states. At the same time, ICCO disbursements in the Northern states (covering three of the five priority states) show an increase.

Interestingly, the South Asia Desk also provides an overview of the strengths and weaknesses of ICCO's work in India. The strong points mentioned include the substantial number and diversity of counterparts, the emphasis on empowerment by many of these counterparts, the 'active dialogue between ICCO and various counterparts on self-reliance, gender, sustainable income security, and sustainable land use', and the openness to 'consider organisations as a whole' and not only specific projects. Obviously, looking at the latter issue, ICCO has taken the internal evaluation of 1988 very seriously. At the same time, some weaknesses show that there always remains a substantial part that lags behind and is in practice extremely difficult to implement. This, for instance, applies to the still 'limited insight of ICCO and [counterparts] in the impact [...] and sustainability of the supported programmes'. Other main weak points of ICCO's work in India, according to ICCO itself, are a 'big regional spread, making networking of NGDOs and joint actions/advocacy more difficult', 'unclear policies with regard to, among other things self-reliance, environment and human rights', the 'ad hoc approach in involving consultants', and 'the limited funds available to enter into collaboration with for ICCO new NGDOS' (ICCO, 1998).

The 1998 Policy Profile ends with an overview of perhaps a bit more realistic (policy) priorities upto the year 2002. Many of these 'priorities' are a repetition of earlier ones. ICCO again emphasises the empowerment approach with the ultimate aim of self-reliance of community organisations and calls for continued attention for the environment, human rights and the capacities of counterparts 'to plan and implement relevant programmes in a difficult and changing context' (ICCO, 1998: 11). Repetition can also be observed with regard to the thematic priorities, sustainable income security and sustainable land use. Basic needs (i.e. education and health- care) are more strongly emphasised than in 1993. The regional policy still mentions the same states as priority, consolidation or withdrawal states. However, a fourth 'regional' category has been added, giving priority to 'national organisations working on thematic priorities like agriculture, environment, forestry, gender, health and NGDO management'. Furthermore, a consolidation of the partner network at around 100 organisations and a slight increase in disbursements are announced. Some of the 'other plans' mentioned in the Policy Profile concern an expansion of the pool of consultants (particularly in the fields of sustainable income security, gender, environment and urban poverty alleviation) and workshops on such issues as gender, self-reliance of community organisations and alternative ways of funding sustainable land use programmes.

Concluding remarks

The above-mentioned observations regarding the ICCO financing in India cannot simply be extended to ICCO's performance in other countries and/or the activities of other Western funding agencies. As the policy and project processing of other country units within ICCO are quite similar to those of the India desk, the observations might apply to ICCO's activities in other countries as well.[29]

To relate the observations to the programmes of the other Dutch MFOs (Cordaid, Hivos and Novib) reference can be made to the final report of the Impact Study published in 1991. Although no firm pronouncements are made about the percentage of 'failed' projects of the four MFOs, it is stated that the survey reveals 'no total failures or cases of corruption or total successes' (Steering Committee Impact Study, 1991: 45). Besides, the Impact Study Steering Committee seriously questions the duration of particularly the economic programmes carried out under the Co-financing Programme.

This general conclusion of the Impact Study also applies to the projects financed by Cordaid, Hivos, Novib and ICCO in India. On the one hand there are deeply involved organisations with limited overheads which systematically carry out relevant programmes targeting the poor; on the other hand, there are NGDOs that have grown (too) fast, which are inadequately equipped to perform activities in different fields and have a poor conception of the 'wider context' in which the projects are situated. The range of the many activities is frequently limited and, although there is certainly progress in some areas, many programme components are not viable in the longer term (Teerink, Viegas & Schenk-Sandbergen, 1991; Shah, 1991).

The optimism about the relevance, efficiency and effectiveness of NGDOs within the sector itself as well as with the Indian Government should be put into perspective (also see Epilogue below). The question should be more seriously raised whether NGDOs present an alternative for the government in the implementation of poverty alleviation programmes. It is not suggested that the NGDO sector in India could not play a role in these programmes. However, the present realities about the functioning of NGDOs in India should be taken into consideration. The recorded problems of accountability, lack of evaluation and research, and leadership and staff problems are just some of the 'pillars of weakness' (Clark, 1991: 63-73). Moreover, for ideological reasons it may not be desirable to create a 'parallel government' which is controlled by only a limited number of people and lacks the mechanisms for accountability to either the government, the own constituency and/or the urban and rural poor in India.

Epilogue

The number of publications on NGDOs and their role in international development cooperation is rapidly growing. The messages they convey range from quite optimistic (Korten, 1990; Clark, 1991) to very critical (Sogge, 1996; Achterhuis; 1993; VandePitte; 1994). The latter are more based on personal experiences than on thorough research. Apart from some general sketches of donor NGDOs, which has been called the 'charity business' (Smith, 1990; Burnell, 1991; Lloyd 1993), in recent years some broad-based evaluation studies of NGDOs have been undertaken. Some by donor NGDOs themselves (Steering Committee Impact Study 1991), some by evaluation desks of bilateral aid agencies (Riddell, 1993), some by independent research institutes (Farrington & Bebbington, 1993; Riddell & Robinson, 1992, 1995), some by bringing together independent researchers (Edwards & Hulme, 1992, 1996; Hulme & Edwards, 1997a), and some by independent researchers alone (Schulpen, 1997; Put, 1998; Arts, 1998; Biekart, 1999). Box 3 provides an overview of a selection of these studies and their major findings.

According to Edwards & Hulme (1995: 6-9) the conclusions drawn from existing studies show that NGDOs 'do not perform as effectively as had been assumed in terms of poverty-reach, cost-effectiveness, sustainability, popular participation (including gender), flexibility and innovation'. Riddell & Robinson (1992) previously established that most of the projects of the NGDOs they examined – multilateral and bilateral projects – 'failed to reach the very poorest'. They concluded that in most cases 'improvement in economic status was modest' and that NGDO interventions can be 'costly to implement [while] benefits take time to mature'. They further stated that 'cost-benefit analysis appears novel to NGDOs', and that 'relatively few projects demonstrated the potential to continue once the NGDO ceased operating in the area'. Nevertheless, about three-quarters of NGDO projects and programmes, they analysed, met their objectives.

The Impact Study of the Dutch Co-financing Programme (Steering Committee Impact Study, 1991) reached similar conclusions. The contribution to poverty alleviation of the examined NGDO programmes was, partly due to limited funding, not very large; people's participation was absent in many projects; cost-awareness was low; and evaluation and monitoring policies were inadequate or absent. Although the effects of the provision of social services were limited as well, the organisations carrying out the projects were successful, professional and had small overheads. Agricultural and credit programmes had a positive impact on incomes and employment. Furthermore, in some instances NGDOs substantially contributed to the organisation of target groups and political change.

Farrington & Bebbington (1993), in a major research project of over sixty case studies on (innovative) NGDOs and sustainable agricultural development, concluded that indeed NGDOs were much better equipped than government research and extension services to be innovative and successful in agrarian projects. They hold wider views on agricultural and technology, are often aware of the possibilities of interaction between livestock, crops and trees, and they take external conditions such as land tenure, organisation and education more into account. In addition, NGDOs often promote participatory methods of problem diagnosis and technology testing. Still, the impact was considered to be small, scaling up turned out to be difficult, evaluation of monitoring by the NGDOs was weak and it was not easy to assess cost and benefits.

As to political reform (the promotion of democracy through participation and empowerment), the contribution of NGDOs seems limited as well, thus making their relevance for civil society building questionable at least (Biekart 1999). The same applies to international lobbying and advocacy as appears from a recent study by Arts (1998), using the 1992 UNCED Conference in Rio de Janeiro as a case in point.

Fowler and Biekart (1996) provide an overview of donor NGDO evaluations, the outcomes of which, however, 'must be treated with caution, if not a pinch of academic salt'. Nevertheless, these studies in general confirm the findings of other studies and add some new insights, for instance the lack of co-ordination between NGDOs, doubts about awareness-raising programmes generating a significant change in power relations, and income-generating activities generally having little impact. Moreover, a recent study comparing Dutch bilateral aid with the assistance from one of the Dutch co-financing organisations to India found that both channels are equally (un)successful in contributing to poverty reduction (Schulpen, 1997 - also see Chapter 3).

Box 3 : NGDO studies and their major findings

Study:

Bering, E. et. al. (1989). Danish NGDOS in India, Tanzania, Zimbabwe, West Africa, Central America, Southern Africa, relief assistance and human rights. Number of case studies: 14.

Findings:

- Danish NGOs are qualified partners in development cooperation; they supplement and complement the work done in official development assistance; they are able to stimulate small-scale development;
- In Latin America and Asia Danish NGOs increasingly move their role away from being implementers to funders of local NGOs; in Africa this picture is mixed;
- A framework agreements is needed with bigger NGOs;
- It has been difficult for DANIDA to be involved in anti-apartheid and human rights projects;

- Selection of partners by Danish NGOs is often based on insufficient knowledge;
- Traditional NGOs are often more less action oriented and are not seeing projects in a wider context; this is particularly the case for some child-oriented NGOs;
- Danish NGOs have difficulties to monitor or actively follow funded projects.

Study:
Dutch Impact Study (1991). Impact of the Dutch co-financing organisations (MFOs) on target groups in developing countries. Number of case studies: 16.

Findings:
- Country policy papers are an important element in developing and evaluating CFO policy;
- MFOs are too reactive in the policy orienting process and have a limited analysing capacity;
- All MFOs have a hardly overlapping portfolio of counterparts with which relations are often long-lasting. The room for renewing this portfolio is limited;
- New funds should mainly be used to increase the number of relationships with African NGOs and to strengthen the quality of African organisations;
- MFOs have rather pretentious formulated objectives with regard to the relation with counterparts (i.e., partnership);
- Most projects and programmes supported by the MFOs are clearly aimed at the poor;
- 'one-dimensional' projects are more successful than integrated, multi-dimensional projects;
- support to 'social provisions' are reasonably effective, whereas economic projects are hardly sustainable nor replicable.

Study:
Carroll, T.F. (1992). Intermediary NGOs and their grassroots interventions, particularly in Latin America. Number of case studies: 30 good performers.

Findings:
- NGOs supporting grassroots organisations are more effective in achieving participation for their beneficiaries and more policy relevant than formal membership organisations;
- They have expanded the organisation of poor people beyond traditional class-based or functional organisations;
- There is a shift to more pragmatic and sustainable development strategies;
- Problems in social service provision by NGOs revolve around minimum standards, cost-effectiveness, affordability and cost recovery;
- The promotion of productive activities is more complicated and failure-prone; the necessity of lowering costs and promoting sustainability lays an excessive burden on family labour.

Study:
Riddell & Robinson (1992). Case studies on poverty reduction in Bangladesh, India, Zimbabwe and Uganda. Number of case studies: 16.

Findings:
Projects are more successful when
1. Objectives correspond to the priorities of the poor and intended beneficiaries are regularly consulted and involved in decision-making at all stages of the project-cycle;
2. Leadership is strong and competent. Excessive centralisation in decision-making, however, undermines staff commitment and limits the potential impact of the intervention;
3. Staff is well trained and educated, and motivated by a reasonable level of remuneration and decent working conditions.

Other findings include:
- The majority of projects examined broadly achieved their objectives and had a positive impact in alleviating poverty;
- Most projects failed to reach the very poorest, and even in cases where poverty alleviation occurred, improvement in economic status was modest;
- Interventions are costly to implement and benefits take time to mature;
- Relatively few of the projects demonstrated the potential to continue once the NGO ceased operating in the area.

Study:
Farrington & Bebbington (1993). NGDOs and sustainable agricultural development in three continents. Number of case studies: more than 60.

Findings:
- NGOs were much better equipped than government research and extension services to be innovative and successful in agrarian projects;
- NGOs hold wider views on agricultural and technology, they are often aware of the possibilities of interaction between livestock, crops and trees and they take wider conditions like land tenure, organisation and education more into account;
- NGOs often have a strong emphasis on participatory methods of problem diagnosis and technology testing;
- The impact was considered to be small, scaling up turned to be difficult;
- Evaluation of monitoring by the NGDOs was weak and it was difficult to assess cost and benefits.

Study:
Riddell et.al. (1994). Finnish-supported projects in Ethiopia, Nepal, Nicaragua and Uganda. Number of case studies: 29.

Findings:

- Overall development impact justifies funding of NGOs; some NGO work of a very high calibre. Still the impact remains small in view of the overall problems of poverty and underdevelopment;
- Particularly primary health care programmes have gained reputation for their quality of service, innovativeness and/or impact;
- NGO performance varies – sometimes greatly – from project to project;
- The ability of Finnish NGOs to articulate their concern for participation, gender and sustainable development has exceeded their ability to bring these concerns into practice;
- NGOs often work in harsh environments in which it is time-consuming, expensive and difficult to achieve results;
- NGOs have been weak in systematising and learning from their experiences.

Study:
Schulpen, L. (1997). Drinking water and irrigation projects in India – comparison of Dutch bilateral aid. Number of case studies: 5 private and 6 bilateral projects.

Findings:

- Both types of donors emphasise the political dimension of poverty reduction (and thus an empowerment approach) in their policy but revert to traditional beneficiary or target group participation in practice;
- The room for manoeuvre (i.e. for following their own policy guidelines) was restricted in practice. In the case of the private aid agency mainly because of internal reasons such as a tendency to regard counterparts as organisations with a high level of autonomy and to a lack of monitoring and evaluation capabilities;
- More structural attention to software aspects such as participation, organisation, education and awareness building produces greater impact of development interventions;
- Both types of donors have financed projects in which greater attention has been paid to software aspects (and as a consequence have had an impact on poverty reduction) and both have also financed projects in which attention to software aspects was minimal. Following this it is concluded that the choice of the aid channel makes no difference in practice.

Study:
Put, M. (1998). Dryland agriculture in Andra Pradesh. Number of case studies: 2 governmental and 1 NGO project.

Findings:

- NGO (AWARE) used an integrated approach of motivation and a combined strategy to assist target groups as well as a parallel and an access strategy;
- NGO was innovative in the sense that it tried to strengthen target groups;
- There was a heavy dependency on a charismatic leader; staff was less

committed and motivated;

- Participatory and democratic mechanisms were restricted; 'empowerment' appeared to be a catchword only;
- NGO was more effective in organising farmers than government programme, but lacking in accountable leadership and internal democracy.

Study:
Arts, B. (1999). (International) political influence of NGDOs in climate and biodiversity arenas. Number of case studies: n.a.

Findings:

- NGOs make some difference in global treaty formation and implementation, although certainly not in all cases. The extent of their political influence should not be overrated and is limited to only a few policy issues;
- The political influence of NGOs is mainly dependent on their own expertise, the attitude and conduct of (like-minded) states, the substance of current environmental regimes, and the nature of intergovernmental negotiations;
- NGOs may increase their political influence, mainly through professionalising their lobbying and advocacy in political arenas and through organising moderate protest outside.

Study:
Biekart, K. (1999). Support to civil society building and democratisation in Honduras, El Salvador and Guatamala. Number of case studies: 4.

Findings:

- It is extremely difficult to attribute the achievements of local intermediary alliances to particular private aid interventions;
- National contexts overwhelmingly determine the outcome of aid interventions;
- Private aid agencies can particularly make a difference in early transition stages by supporting broad alliances in civil society capable of performing an intermediary role in political society;
- Only few private aid agencies systematically analyse the local political and economic context prior to intervention, and the choice of the moment of intervention for 'tipping the balance' towards democratic transition was (thus) accidental rather than a deliberate strategy;
- The comparative advantages of private aid agencies over official aid agencies are that the former have the capacity to react quickly to Southern demands, they provide modest amounts of financial aid adapted to carefully identified needs with a minimum of conditions attached, they work in close coordination with other agencies and local actors, and they combine financial and non-financial support.

Study:
ABOS (1999). Partnership relations of Belgian NGDOs in 26 countries. Number of case studies: 85 NGOs.

Findings:

- Partners are chosen more on basis of general knowledge or recommendations than on preliminary research;
- Most funding goes to health and education. and to a lesser extent to agriculture, economic and rural development;
- Results are in general positive, but the lack of regional and sectoral co-ordination hamper impact.

Study:

Oakley, P. (1999). Danish NGDO impact study (with case studies in Bangladesh, Tanzania and Nicaragua. Number of case studies: 45 projects.

Findings:

Strengths of project interventions of Danish NGOs

- Danish NGOs appear to have focused consistently and with effect on poverty, in its broadest sense;
- Danish NGOs have managed to build up an association with a committed, resourceful and dependable body of Southern partners;
- The absence of any abject 'failures' reinforces the perception that the Danish NGOs are quite thorough in the ways in which they maintain contact and support projects and are in a position to know their current status;
- Danish support to basic services is well founded and widely appreciated for its timeliness and the care with which it is given;
- Danish NGOs have a widely recognised role in supporting civil society organisations to participate in wider movements aiming at state and policy reform.

Weaknesses of project interventions of Danish NGOs

- Danish NGOs are generally weak on the broader contextual analysis;
- Most of the individual project reports suggested that Monitoring and Evaluation system was inadequate, in some cases alarmingly too;
- Danish NGO staff are generally not strong technically on many theoretical, methodological and operational aspects of development interventions;
- A 'wider perspective' and a conscious effort to assess the project work in the light of national level policies is lacking (mainly Bangladesh and Tanzania);
- Level of practice among Danish NGOs of what is fashionably termed 'participatory development' is not very high.

Source: Hoebink and Schulpen, 1999: 5-9.

NOTES

1. The only NGDO regarded more sceptically was the Action for Integrated Rural Development Society (AIRDS) (see Schulpen, 1997). Novib also discussed the BINGOs. In 1988, a report entitled Big and Still Beautiful

(Beets, Neggers and Wils, 1988) came to a very positive conclusion with regard to the involvement of the target group in BINGO programmes. These large NGDOs have 'kept their flexibility, participation and closeness to the poor while having wider impact and being considerably less bureaucratic and corrupt than government services'.

2. Within ICCO the discussion on BINGOs concentrated on the organisational consequences for ICCO itself. The ICCO Asia desk, in a reaction to the proposal for financing of BINGOs, stated that the 'financial need of these [BINGOs] has increased over the years' and that 'in general, this growing demand is justified, considering the expertise of these organisations, the management qualities, the degree of poverty of the target group and the development approach.' In the policy paper entitled ICCO op weg naar het jaar 2000 (ICCO on its way to 2000) BINGOs were an issue. In this paper ICCO announced that, in the context of the proposal, it would strive towards a network of some 50 organisations in the Third World, which eventually would receive a minimum of 50 per cent of the ICCO budget.
3. In the 1986 ICCO Annual Report (ICCO, 1987b), it was mentioned that 'counterparts which have been active since the mid-1970s in rural development are successful and working on a large scale [...] It has become clear that ICCO should not work any longer on the basis of project-financing with organisations with an (area-wise) extended approach.' Instead of funding per project, programme financing and organisation financing were seen as more appropriate in these cases. The remark that rural development BINGOs should be supported over a longer period with funding secured for upto three years was lagging behind the actual practice of ICCO in India.
4. It was hoped that with responsibility for the whole project/programme cycle, from application to evaluation, vested in one person financial matters would take less time so that more time could be spent on the programme itself during visits.
5. The concept of empowerment is here described as a contribution to strengthening the limited power of the poor masses to control and influence government due to 'various, interdependent factors: low level of literacy and awareness, inability to organise themselves into effective pressure groups, lack of sustenance power due to poor health conditions, low income, uncertainty of income and large scale unemployment'. What is basically captured here under the term 'empowerment' is the same as what was captured in previous reports and papers under such terms as participation, structural change or political development.
6. The discussion on BINGOs initiated by the ICCO director in 1986 led to intense debates both for fear of pressure on the small(er) projects and more bureaucracy, and the assumptions underlying the BINGO proposal (i.e., 'big agencies can perhaps better organise masses on a larger scale and thus influence power-relationships on a higher political level than smaller organisations; some economic problems require a co-ordinated approach on a larger scale' (Beets, Neggers & Wils, 1988)). In the later withdrawn ICCO policy paper ICCO op weg naar het jaar 2000 (ICCO, 1989), the discussion

was brought to a more general level. It was proposed to work towards the building of a worldwide network of 50 so-called key partners to receive at least 50 per cent of the regular ICCO funds. The financing of the BINGOs and particularly the demands with regard to the large NGDOs were further discussed at the India desk in 1990/1991.

7. A sharp decrease in the number of projects was only possible by reducing the number of counterparts. Over the period 1990-1992, a large number of relationships were indeed terminated in 'view of the present and future staff capacity of the India team' (ICCO, 1993b: 12). Of course, relationships with counterparts in India have been terminated ever since the start of ICCO's involvement in 1971. Only a few of the organisations supported in the 1970s survived the 1980s as ICCO counterparts. Nevertheless, an increasing part of the funds available for India each year have been absorbed by already existing counterparts. It is for this reason that new applicants for an ICCO grant over the last couple of years have received a standard letter in which it is indicated that 'almost the total annual budget of ICCO for the Indian subcontinent is being utilised for the financing of follow-up proposals' from existing counterparts and that 'there is in general only a relatively very small amount [...] available to enter into collaboration with new projects' (ICCO, standard letter to turn down new applications).
8. Due to ICCO's financial problems during 1989/1990 the India desk already pursued a policy of tight financing.
9. More concrete policy proposals were to be written in the years to follow on issues such as human rights, land reform, communalism/fundamentalism, ecology and sustainable agriculture, income-generating projects and the ecumenical network in India. Separate papers were indeed prepared on some of these topics, including urban poverty, in 1990.
10. Wherever possible data cover the period 1971-1993. For some of the items (notably those discussed in the section 'type of projects' and 'target group') data is only available for the period upto 1990. The empirical data, and the categorisation, were derived from ICCO's internal data. The authors thank Mr. H. Rijpkema for his assistance in the input and processing of the data.
11. These projects are frequently carried out by organisations working directly for a specific target group. There are also (support) organisations which offer their services to other private development organisations.
12. These are also the states from which ICCO received (and rejected) the majority of project proposals ICCO (see also Chapter 3).
13. Half of the projects (395) did not provide an own contribution in cash. During the period 1971-1990 the number of projects per year with no own cash contribution did not decrease. In 1990 also, when the India desk insisted on a substantial own contribution, such a contribution is not mentioned in half of the projects. This does not imply, however, that there was no substantial own contribution in the form of, for example, voluntary labour or goods.
14. From 1978 a total of 108 so-called additional projects of the India desk of ICCO were approved, of which 57 by the European Community (EC) and 51 by the Dutch government. By far the majority of the EC projects (84 per cent)

were so-called 'block grants': projects with a maximum duration of one year and an average contribution of about NLG 17,000, particularly for the purchase of materials. The India desk often used these block grant projects as a first financial assistance to new counterparts. The major part of the projects funded by the Dutch government were emergency aid projects and agricultural development programmes. The sudden cut off of SP contributions in 1993 was mainly due to a sharp increase in emergency aid by the Dutch government itself, leaving less extra funds available for the co-financing organisations.

15. The decline and subsequent stagnation of the allocation of funds by the India desk in 1989 and 1990 resulted from the disappearance of a large number of prominent counterparts with a great absorption capacity; the rather permanent devaluation of the rupee which was much higher than the inflation; the requirement of a substantial local contribution (from the government, a bank or the target group) as from 1990; and the fact that ICCO's largest counterpart in India, AWARE, (temporarily) needed less financial assistance. Moreover, the India desk did not always have sufficient manpower due to high turnover of staff.
16. In the beginning of the 1990s some new sectors were introduced in the ICCO administration. 'Primary productive sector' basically covers the old sector 'economic and industrial activity', whereas 'organisation building' was a sub-sector of 'general activities'. The latest new sector – community work – should probably replace 'community development'.
17. The decision of the India desk in the early 1990s to 'rejuvenate' its counterpart pool (i.e. the termination of the relationship with a large number of NGDOs and a more active acquisition of new organisations) did not meet the expectations. In 1993 still only 15 per cent of the projects were registered as 'new'. Together they accounted for 9.7 per cent of the total ICCO contribution to projects in India (see also Chapter 3).
18. In this context project financing refers to, in principle, the financing of a once-only activity, while programme financing refers to the financing of a continuous, not exactly time-bound programme.
19. With the 23 new counterparts of 1991-1993, ICCO had a (financial) relationship with a total number of 283 NGDOs over the period 1971-1993. On average, each of these NGDOs had 3.4 projects approved by ICCO. In reality nearly 40 per cent of the NGDOs had only one project sanctioned, whereas 17 per cent 'scored' over six projects.
20. Christian-secular organisations are secular organisations that have no links with one of the Protestant Churches in India, but do operate on the basis of Biblical inspiration. All organisations supported by ICCO are secular at the implementation level.
21. Programme evaluations, in which through field visits to a limited number of counterparts one or two themes are looked into in more detail, are conducted by the Dutch government and an MFO jointly. In 1982 ICCO's India programme was evaluated in this way (see: Buck, 1982). The central themes were the participation of the target group in programmes and the transfer of authority from ICCO to the counterpart. In May 1991, a new DGIS/ICCO

programme evaluation of the India programme was carried out. This time the focus was on 'sustainable agriculture' (Chandy *et.al.*, 1991). The Impact Study (1991) is of a more general nature.

22. An exception must be made here for the so-called block grant projects of the European Community which are often not evaluated as positive.
23. In well-organised organisations the staff charged with financial affairs are classified in a separate structure and systematic budget control and regular inspection by a chartered accountant takes place. In weaker organisations corruption often occurs.
24. Dr. N.C.B. Nath, chairman of the consultancy organisation FAIR (New Delhi) also emphasises the importance of 'a congruent development philosophy, technical competence and skills, acceptance by the grassroots workers and necessary research and management skills', as conditions for justified intervention (see: Nath, 1989).
25. In the introduction of an evaluation report Ms. M. Mukhopadya describes this problem as follows: 'The impact of financial assistance from international NGOs on the voluntary movement in India has both served a useful purpose and in many ways derailed the movement ... The negative outcome of such assistance has been the artificial growth of voluntary organizations, because money was available for the mushrooming of leadership which has no commitment to societal change, the corruption of ordinary field workers who do not have to exercise public accountability for the funds received to people in their own environment, the growing tendency to concentrate power and resources - power that flows controlling large funds ...'.
26. In this connection it should be noted that within ICCO the division of work between the so-called project promotion staff (preparation of new funding applications) and the monitoring staff (charged with monitoring the projects in implementation) was changed in order to integrate the learning experiences regarding both phases and to achieve greater continuity in project processing.
27. The above implies that with unchanged allocation to fewer counterparts a greater turnover can be achieved by increasing the average ICCO funding, or by granting large subsidies to a limited number of large NGOs (the so-called BINGOs). In order to be able to continue to honour the relatively small applications of the often beginning small organisations, the latter option has been chosen. In this context it must be noted that a causal relationship was observed between the size of an organisation, ICCO financing and the efficiency and/or quality of the work performed (compare: Beets, Neggers and Wils 1988).
28. During the 1990s, the India desk was replaced by the South Asia Desk comprising, besides India, Sri Lanka, Bangladesh, Pakistan and Nepal.
29. This observation agrees with the pronouncements by the then managing director of ICCO who in 1988 created quite a stir by saying in a newspaper interview that he would be content if 50 per cent of the development projects are really successful. By that he did not mean that the other 50 per cent is wasted, but that its effect is not immediately obvious.

3

POVERTY, PARTICIPATION AND EMPOWERMENT : Examples of Dutch Development Policy in India

— Lau Schulpen

In the Netherlands private development organisations and the government provide financial support to non-governmental development organisations (NGDOs)in the South. This chapter reviews the India policies of the Dutch Ministry for Development Cooperation and the non-governmental development organisation ICCO, and examines their effectiveness in reaching the poor in India.

Developments in international and Dutch development policies

October 1999 marked the fiftieth anniversary of development cooperation, an event which was commemorated in the Netherlands – and, most probably, in other countries as well. A post-Second World War phenomenon, development aid in many respects has ameliorated the problem of poverty in the world. However, development aid has not always been effective and there are as many stories of successful aid as there are of failures. Especially in the last decade the question of how to improve the effectiveness of aid provision has often been posed. How can we make development aid serve its primary goal of poverty alleviation more effectively? This question is certainly not new and a variety of answers have been forwarded in the past.

One of the more recent contributions to the ongoing discussion concerning the quality of development aid comes from the World Bank. In Assessing Aid (World Bank, 1998), researchers of one of the biggest multilateral donor agencies make some very interesting and radical recommendations. The major recommendation is that aid should be concentrated as much as possible in countries with sound policy and good governance because the effect of development aid on poverty alleviation in these countries is far more profound. Furthermore, aid to these countries could be provided far more easily. As recipient countries are highly capable of defining and implementing their own policies, it is no longer necessary that projects are dictated by the will of donor agencies. Donor agencies are requested to supply the financial means for these policies and this can be done more easily through programme or budget support.

In a nutshell, these ideas of the World Bank influenced Dutch policy. The coalition agreement of the second social-democratic and liberal cabinet (the so-called Purple Cabinet) stated with regard to development cooperation that the distribution of bilateral aid 'will be based on sound policy, including economic policy and good governance, according to international standards'. Soon after she took office in 1998, the present Minister of Development Cooperation Ms Herfkens announced a policy review. The number of aid-receiving countries, which had grown to 119 during the term of her predecessor Pronk, was to be drastically reduced. To justify her policy reform Herfkens could refer to the earlier-mentioned World Bank study which concluded that 'efforts to "buy" policy improvements in countries where there is no movement for reform [...] have typically failed' (World Bank, 1998: 3). Herfkens' efforts to reduce the number of aid recipients have resulted in a list of 19 countries with which the Netherlands will establish long-term bilateral relationships. Such bilateral aid will allow a more prominent role for other forms of support, a shift that had already been proposed by her predecessor to improve development cooperation (Ministerie van Buitenlandse Zaken, 1996).

In an effort to improve the quality of Dutch development aid, Herfkens also took action in other areas. A critical report on the multilateral channel, including the development cooperation programme of the European Union (EU), was finalised in 1999 (Ministerie van Buitenlandse Zaken, 1999a). Although conclusions about future outcomes carry a positive note, the report also clearly hints at the wish for a reduced Dutch contribution to the programme (which in practice would be almost impossible). Herfkens also focused her attention on the third channel for development cooperation, the private channel, which in the Netherlands is particularly represented by four co-financing organisations: ICCO, Novib, Cordaid and Hivos.

The co-financing programme and co-financing organisations

The Dutch co-financing programme (MFP) dates back to December 1994, when the then Under-secretary of Foreign Affairs announced that for assistance to less developed countries an amount of NLG five million will be made available for co-financing by the government of development projects of non-commercial private organisations'. The lobby of mainly Catholic and Protestant circles had paid off and in the years to follow the MFP became a small, but regular part of the Dutch budget for development cooperation. The initial NLG five million raised to NLG 416 million in 1994. After a few years the programme was streamlined and the funds were spent through three (later four and from 2000 onwards five) mediating or co-financing organisations (MFOS, see Box).

In the 35 years of their existence the MFOs have succeeded in creating for themselves ever more room for manoeuvre. Formally, this has been laid down in the 1980 Programme Financing Agreement between the then Minister of Development Cooperation and MFOs, and which has been renewed every four years since. MFOs are given an annual block grant (independent spending with accountability for the entire amount of money). Although they already had a certain degree of freedom to develop their own policies, they were in a better position to implement these policies as they could make decisions on the projects and programmes which they financed.

The block grant was introduced without an evaluation of the programme had taken place. Apparently, Dutch politicians were so convinced of the competency of the MFOs that a formal assessment was considered unnecessary. MFOs fuelled this conviction by promoting themselves as the primary channel for poverty reduction. Even after an Impact Study conducted in 1991 unexpectedly presented a less favourable picture, they persisted in their conviction, though in a more modest way. By structurally increasing the MFO budget in the 1990s, Dutch politics actually reaffirmed this conviction.

The co-financing organisations

The amount of money available for the Co-financing Programme (MFP) has to be split between four, and since January 2000 five, MFOs. In 1999, the Catholic organisation Cordaid (formerly CEBEMO) and the Protestant ICCO, which equally shared the NLG five million in 1965, each received 25% of the funds. Novib (secular) received 33% and Hivos (humanistic) 17%. The latter two and Foster Parents Plan Netherlands, which shares in the funds from 2000, acquire substantial additional funds through fund-raising activities among the general public.

Since its start in 1965, the MFP has grown substantially: from 2 per cent of the Dutch budget for development cooperation to 6.5% in 1992. Based on the results of the so-called Impact Study, an evaluation of the Co-financing Programme which was presented in 1991, the Ministry for Development Cooperation (DGIS) raised the funds for co-financing to 7 per cent in 1994 and further to 10 per cent in 1998. In addition to these regular Dutch government funds, the MFOs also utilise so-called additional funds from the European Union.

Between 1986 and 1994, the MFOs approved 20,035 new projects (ICCO 29 per cent, CEBEMO 44.6 per cent, Novib 18.3 per cent and Hivos 8.1 per cent. In 1980, CEBEMO was active in 74 Third World countries, ICCO in 64; Novib in 31 and Hivos in 24. In 1989, these numbers had grown in particular for ICCO (93) and Novib (52). In the early 1990s, however, there was a substantial decline resulting from stricter concentration policies. In

1994 ICCO had reduced the number of countries to 53, CEBEMO to 63 an Novib to 47. Only Hivos showed an increase: from 24 countries at the end of the 1980s to 29 in 1994.

In line with her efforts to streamline bilateral aid (concerning countries, interventions, sectors) Herfkens initiated discussions with the four co-financing organisations (MFOs) in order to arrive at a division of tasks between the Ministry for Development Cooperation (DGIS) and the MFOs, and thereby maximise the efforts in the fight against poverty. In order to enhance the quality of aid rendered, it was thus considered important that these two channels for assistance are geared to one another, something that had often been missing in the past (see, among others, Schulpen, 1998). This applies, of course, in the first instance to the selected countries where both DGIS and MFOs are actively involved and where, according to the minister, the latter should focus particularly on 'the mobilisation and support of civilians living in poverty and the building of institutional capacity' (Ministerie van Buitenlandse Zaken, 1999b). Furthermore, the minister suggested that MFOs concentrate especially on those countries where it is more difficult for the Dutch government to fight poverty, in instances where they are a little wealthier or where good governance or policy is lacking. In the first discussions that took place the MFOs expressed their willingness to collaborate in the proposed coordination.

Initially, the MFOs were somewhat on the defence because they feared losing their independence. They were not completely wrong, as in Herfkens' conception the MFOs are part of the Dutch framework of (bilateral) aid for which her ministry provides most of the funds and therefore is responsible. In contrast to her predecessors, she is less inclined towards a hands-off attitude where MFOs are concerned.

ICCO and DGIS in India: from policy to project

Are MFOs indeed more successful in reaching the poor than the

Dutch government? To answer this question it should first be made more specific: has the co-financing organisation ICCO been more successful in reaching the poor in India than the Dutch government in the period 1971-1992? In view of the fact that both channels list (sustainable) poverty alleviation as their main goal, framing the question in such a specific way is justified. Moreover, for both the Dutch government and ICCO India has been a major, if not the major, aid-receiving country. Between 1971 and 1992 Dutch bilateral aid to India amounted to almost NLG four billion. An additional NLG 208 million were supplied by ICCO. Most of the projects supported by this organisation were in India and they absorbed more than half of its budget. As for Dutch bilateral aid, India has for many years been the major recipient (one of the three main aid-receiving countries). The fact that foreign aid at present is only of minor importance to India does not change this. The question whether Dutch aid has contributed to the improvement of the living conditions of the poor in India requires a closer look from the perspective of both policy and implementation of DGIS' and ICCO's aid to India.

Overall policy

The slogan 'The Netherlands as a guiding light' is hardly pertinent to the Dutch poverty policy. The Dutch government tended to follow (in particular initiators such as the World Bank and UNDP) rather than shape international policy. This does not mean that there is nothing original in Dutch poverty policy. Most of the 'original policy developments', however, are rather recent, as for instance the reassessment of the foreign policy in the 1990s (see also Hoebink and Schulpen, 1998). In general, Dutch policy reflects international thinking about development and poverty alleviation. Briefly, this means more policy orientation towards poverty reduction, basic needs and participation in the 1970s, return to economic growth (under the term 'indirect poverty reduction' linked to the retreat of the state and more attention for private initiatives in the 1980s, renewed attention for poverty reduction and participation (under the term 'human development') from the late 1980s onwards and a search for a synthesis between economic growth and poverty reduction (including democratisation) from the mid-1990s onwards.

The MFOs do not show a similar change in policy. In fact, there was hardly any policy development at all before 1974. Discussions mostly focused on an increase in financial means for MFOs and the slow manner in which the government processed project proposals from MFOs. Discussions in 1974 resulted in a number of agreements on policy. With social justice and self-reliance as their major objectives, the MFOs agreed on a target group policy. Among other things the MFOs indicated that they would prioritise initiatives from the target group, activities that encourage local leadership, activities with high local costs and activities directed at enhancing self-reliance of the target group in economic, political and socio-cultural respects.

Linked to an integrated approach (or better, multi-component approach) the target group approach is still the modus operandi of the MFOs. Although sustainable poverty alleviation formally replaced this approach in the late 1980s and the four MFOs stress different aspects, participation, awareness-raising and organisation have always been the keystones of MFO policy (see, among others, GOM, 1995). It is therefore not surprising that MFOs are promoted – by themselves and others – as a very suitable channel for poverty reduction. Has experience not shown that especially in the context of poverty reduction participation of the target group is of utmost (and sometimes overriding) importance?

India policy

The India policies of the Dutch government and ICCO in many respects reflect, as they should, the above-described overall policy. In the 1970s, after the usual initial problems, DGIS approved the first poverty alleviation projects in India. In the early 1980s a way was sought to broaden the relationship between the Netherlands and India, particularly the economic relations, and in the course of the 1980s women and the environment emerged more manifestly as themes spearheading the Netherlands' India policy. Furthermore, from the late 1980s onwards, DGIS has increasingly emphasised participation, education and organisation of the target group in projects aimed at direct poverty alleviation. In ICCO's India policy the political dimension of development put forward by its India desk was central until the late 1980s when that policy was considerably refined. The principle of the 1970s and 1980s, that the number of supported organisations should only be increased in selected states, was abandoned for completely different and stricter assessment and selection criteria in the late 1980s. The major reason for this shift from 'almost anything is fine' to a more critical attitude is provided by the internal evaluation executed by the India desk. Staff members of the desk characterised 20 per cent of all Indian organisations that had been supported since 1972 as weak or bad, while they were unable to assess 40 per cent of the organisations. There could be no better example of the failure of the selection and monitoring system that had been in use until then.[1]

India as a test case

A major resemblance between the India policies of DGIS and ICCO is that for both donor agencies India was a test case in many instances. For DGIS, for example, this applies to its efforts to broaden its scope of operation in the 1980s when development cooperation was seen as a catalyst for fostering ties with India in other areas. Initiatives were taken especially in the economic field and some agreements on cooperation were signed. However, ties were never really deepened, not even in the economic field. The role of development cooperation as a driving force to cultivate broader relations was therefore not a resounding success.

In some respects India was a guinea pig for ICCO as well. This applies for instance to the support given to so-called non-natural partners (i.e. non-Christian organisations). Almost all the organisations that were supported by ICCO in the 1970s were Christian. This situation had drastically changed by the end of the 1980s when only a quarter of the supported organisations in India could rightly be characterised as Christian. Others were basically secular (see Chapter 2). As to decentralisation and the financing of programmes and organisations, India was a test case for ICCO too. Efforts to enlarge the influence of Southern NGDOs in policy and implementation (i.e. decentralisation) in the early 1980s failed partly due to a lack of interest from these organisations. On the other hand, the financing of programmes and organisations had actually already become part of ICCO's practice in India far before this type of financing became common. This mainly resulted from the fact that the India desk had created its own big organisations that were supported for a long period of time. In essence it concerned project-based financing of programmes and organisations (see also Schulpen & Van der Velden, 1992).

Success and failure go hand in hand

Although the India policies of DGIS and ICCO might be considered rather successful in some fields, they were significantly less so in others. DGIS, for instance, has succeeded in effecting a balance between project and programme support, an exercise which took them a lot of time. The same applies to the concentration on sectors on which finally an agreement was reached in the mid-1980s. Similarly, an agreement was also reached on the concentration of aid in a number of states. The significance of this concentration, however, is questionable. The population of the five states, in which Dutch bilateral aid was concentrated until the late 1990s, was equivalent to the total population of seven other selected countries receiving Dutch bilateral aid (Tanzania, Pakistan, Bangladesh, Sri Lanka, Kenya, Sudan and North Yemen). Besides, the Netherlands spent more than half of its bilateral aid to India outside these selected states which only received the funds allocated to drinking water and irrigation projects. Although DGIS decided to focus on the poorest districts within these states, the drinking water projects in Uttar Pradesh were still spread over 5,000 villages in 14 different districts.

Prompted by the internal evaluation that took place in the 1980s,

ICCO, in turn, succeeded in reducing the number of counterparts substantially in the early 1990s. Between 1989 and 1992 the financial relations with 100 counterparts in India were terminated (see also Chapter 5). Internal factors related with the counterpart, for example doubts about the internal functioning of the counterpart organisation or a lack of transparency observed by ICCO, were the major determinants of the termination in most cases. However, ICCO itself was not entirely clear with its counterparts concerning its reasons for terminating the relationship (see Chapter 5). Clearer guidelines led to changes in for instance the concentration of ICCO support in specific states. On the other hand, there were no major changes in the size of the ICCO-supported NGDOs, despite the policy developed for this purpose. The majority of ICCO's counterparts were, and still are, relatively small organisations in terms of number of staff, turnover and target group.

Limited policy

In general, the India policies of DGIS and ICCO were either often a reflection of on-going practice (and, as such, mainly had an ex-post legitimating function) or they hardly materialised. It therefore seems, certainly in the case of DGIS, that a substantial part of the aid distribution in India deviated from the outlined general policy. This was mainly due to the limited room for manoeuvre for both ICCO and the Dutch government. In the case of ICCO this was partly self-imposed: NGDOs were seen (and dealt with) as, self-reliant and autonomous organisations. However, the Indian rules and regulations, together with constant pressure from the Indian government for programme support, limited the possibilities to shape government policy actively. The same applies to the project level. Genuine participation, aimed at poverty alleviation and organisation of the target group (sometimes called 'software' aspects), are part and parcel of ICCO's operating procedure. For DGIS these aspects have become more important over time, especially in those sectors that are supposed to address poverty alleviation directly, for instance drinking water and irrigation. It was only after a lot of time, however, that DGIS' counterparts accepted these software aspects. At the same time, it appeared that ICCO's counterparts did not always take software aspects seriously. This brings us to discuss projects and implementation.

Drinking water in Darsi

In the Netherlands, one hardly finds fluoride-free toothpaste. Apparently, fluoride helps to protect teeth against decay. In some parts of the world, however, the addition of fluoride is unnecessary as there is already enough fluoride in the drinking water. In some cases the fluoride level is so high that it endangers health. Long-time usage of high-level fluoride drinking water causes illness, lameness and crooked limbs. Relatively large parts of Andra Pradesh are affected by excessive fluoride levels. DGIS therefore was keen to support the proposal to tackle this problem through the construction of a piped water system. In the late 1970s the Dutch government agreed to a project which aimed to provide clean drinking water to 111 villages surrounding the rural town Darsi. Initially, and completely in line with the views at that time, the project was restricted to the construction and installation of the water system. Taking into consideration experiences from other donor agencies with drinking water projects elsewhere in the world, DGIS soon realised that construction alone was not enough. Inhabitants of the area should also be encouraged to indeed use the clean drinking water and maintain the system. Although DGIS could come to an agreement with the Indian government on the necessary awareness-raising activities and activities related to community participation, income generation and organisation of the target group, the implementation of these 'software' aspects subsequently raised a lot of complications and insolvable problems. For instance, the NGDO, recruited to build the toilets, did manage to build the agreed number, but failed to provide the necessary awareness-raising activities and health promotion. For years the toilets built with no housing have stood as silent witnesses in the landscape.

In 1990 the resumption of the 'software' component seemed

to proceed smoothly in the beginning. Although only a small number of the 111 villages were involved, the newly participating organisation certainly made progress. Unfortunately, this progress was temporary. Disagreement between field staff and the coordinating office led to the actual termination of the activities (and the project). As a result, the achievements of the 'software' activities collapsed almost immediately. The organisations of target groups that had been created at village level dissolved within a short period of time or were left in the lurch because field staff were never going to return. In the meantime, the maintenance of the drinking water system left a lot to be desired. It was only at places which were to be visited by dignitaries that the system seemed to function well. In the villages (especially those further away from the main road) there were a lot of breaks in the system. Missing taps on the water tanks caused water to gush through the openings to the extent that the more remote villages were deprived of water. All in all, this was hardly a sustainable project.

Empowerment and irrigation in Guntur

The NGDO Centre for Rural Development (CRD) operates only some tens of kilometres north of Darsi. CRD is one of ICCO's regulars and has been supported since 1983. CRD's programme (with organisation, training, awareness-raising and activities in the field of economic and social development as the main components) at first sight resembles the programmes of many other NGDOs in India. This is also reflected by its primary focus on a specific culturally defined section of the population and the creation of women's, youth and village organisations in the 142 villages in which it is actively involved.

However, a major difference with other NGDOs is the central role of the political dimension in its philosophy and the associated strategy which is expressed in the planning and decision-making process of the organisation. In a nutshell, the strategy comprises the organisation of the target group into separate groups, compulsory interaction and highly active participation of the target group from the very beginning in both decision making and implementation and the acquisition of as much government funds as possible (both individual and group level) for the chosen activities.

CRD has made the use of government funds as a standard for measuring the 'autonomy' of a community. As a rule, the target group is required to try to acquire funds from the various government programmes. To do this the target group not only needs to be informed about government programmes (what funds are available, who they target and how to submit a proposal), its members must also be provided with the skills to engage in the tussle with the government machinery through training, organisation and awareness-raising. Although there is no concrete evidence with regard to corruption in governmental bodies responsible for the implementation of poverty alleviation programmes, there are numerous stories. Almost every villager knows a first-hand story about a beneficiary of such a programme who in the end lost part of the government support to bribe or was left with a white elephant. Besides, the bureaucracy, that is inherent in government programmes, poses enormous problems to illiterate people who have a holy fear for government bodies.

Throughout the years, CRD's target group has frequently managed to benefit from government programmes at all levels: individual (equipment, seeds, fertiliser, cows), small group (irrigation) and community (community homes, electricity, water supply). This, however, does not mean that the acquired assets are always sustainable. For instance, many of the irrigation wells that were built or deepened with government funds do not produce sufficient water for effective irrigation due to a declining groundwater level in recent years. The above notwithstanding, CRD's strategy has on the one hand, created the opportunities for the target group to gain a better understanding of governmental development programmes, and on the other, contributed to the streamlining of these programmes. More important in the long run,

CRD has created the opportunity for the target group to participate in and contribute to these programmes more substantially (see also Chapter 7).

Group or individual in Mahabubnagar

Participation certainly does not characterise the organisation Action for Integrated Rural Development Society (AIRDS) which operates in Mahabubnagar in Andra Pradesh. This NGDO had been supported by ICCO since 1983, but the financial relationship was terminated in the mid-1990s. On paper, AIRDS' activities are to be applauded. Working in 79 communities, AIRDS focuses on the well-known set of three NGDO activities: training, awareness-raising and organisation linked to income-generating activities with the ultimate goal of forging self-reliant village communities.

Particularly where income-generating activities and organisation of the target group are concerned, the NGDO has severely failed. Even after almost eleven years one can hardly speak of any semblance of organisation of the target group, not to mention independently functioning village organisations. In contrast to the outlined strategy for the target group, the economic activities were directed towards individuals and especially towards those who already had some clout within the communities. The revolving fund, that was established to finance the economic activities, functioned only marginally. In the period 1984-1991, 253 loans were granted through this fund, totalling almost Rs three million. In 1991 only Rs 0.8 had been repaid, an amount which is insufficient to service a real revolving fund. Moreover, the funds were not distributed evenly among the target group: only 220 members in 34 communities received loans. As a consequence, AIRDS was seen as a friendly sponsor by part of the target group while the remaining part hardly benefited from its activities.

Spontaneous participation in West Bengal?

Farmers in the northern districts of West Bengal did profit from the activities of a DGIS-supported irrigation project, certainly in the case of the so-called Pump Dug Wells (PDWs) of the North Bengal Terai Development Project. Heavily subsidised by the project, groups of five small farmers purchase a pump which they use and maintain collectively. Not only are these farmers obliged to form small groups, experience with growing vegetables is required, their land must be adjoining, and they have to bear the cost of a quarter of the investments.

Although the project had paid some attention to organisation building, this in practice proved to be unnecessary. The farmers were quite capable of organising themselves, and were able to agree on the financing of their personal contributions and the use and maintenance of the pumps. It was uncommon for them to have the opportunity to irrigate their land at only a quarter of the cost. Several groups even decided to buy a more powerful pump and paid the extra themselves. Although not all participants of the PDW part of the project are small farmers or peasants, they constitute the majority and the project has succeeded in achieving its objectives.

This example clearly shows that to ensure the participation of the target group it is important that the group recognises the benefit. It is, of course, for this reason that the target group (at least the part that qualifies as such) of the AIRDS project participates in the revolving fund. In other words: people participate 'when they are convinced that the benefits outweigh the costs' (Schulpen, 1998: 204). In fact, people's decision to participate in an activity is based on an individual cost-benefit analysis. Moreover, and notwithstanding the fact that spontaneous participation (as in the Terai Project) may occur, experience has shown that private initiatives should not be expected, at least not spontaneously. It is because of this that in most cases the initiative for a participatory approach is taken by the implementing organisation, irrespective of whether it concerns an NGDO, a government agency or a donor agency.

Outsider involvement may therefore be highly important for a participatory approach in a project. At the same time, the above-described examples show that an outsider involvement is hardly any guarantee that the project will be implemented in such a way that stimulates participation, nor that the intervention will lead to poverty alleviation. DGIS made efforts to introduce participatory procedures in the Darsi project, but did not succeed. In spite of its participatory strategy AIRDS was unable to induce participation of the target group, while in the Terai Project participation of the target group was 'spontaneous'. CRD, to conclude, not only succeeded in realising the participation of the target group in the project but also managed to bring about some degree of empowerment through such active participation.

The contractor decides

The above-described examples reinforce the observation that for both DGIS and ICCO the possibilities to focus their projects more directly on poverty depend, to a large extent, on those who actually implement the projects. In other words, DGIS can include software aspects in its policy in order to ensure that its projects for the poor are more sustainable but when the implementing organisations, in this case mostly government departments staffed by engineers, are opposed to such activities, realisation of projects becomes very difficult or impossible. In the case of ICCO, the lack of monitoring and too much (blind) trust in counterparts may lead to long-term support of NGDOs which disregard their own strategy.

It should be mentioned, however, that over the years DGIS has been able to convince its counterparts that a more participatory approach leads to better results. For instance, the first drinking water projects in Uttar Pradesh were simple construction projects. In the mid-1980s the software aspects which were introduced, by trial and error, got accepted gradually. More recent projects include participatory and organisation elements from the very beginning, both on paper and in practice. While DGIS struggled to get its new approach accepted in India (and elsewhere), ICCO internally evaluated the Indian organisations it supported. This finally resulted in the termination of the financial relationship with many of these organisations, as well as the design of clear guidelines and the adoption of a more business-like approach. More attention for, among other things, internal functioning of the counterparts and reporting should provide a better understanding of the partner organisations and reduce the risk of failure. It can therefore be stated that DGIS and ICCO have learnt from the past.

Conclusion

It is praiseworthy that DGIS and ICCO were able to learn from the past. However, is one of these channels more capable than the other to reach the poor? Does ICCO (representing the private channel for development aid) or DGIS (as bilateral donor) contribute best to the mutual aim of sustainable poverty alleviation? With regard to policy DGIS and ICCO have many points in common. Policy-wise, India was a test case for both organisations and their programmes strongly focus on poverty. Although the emphasis on poverty is more clear in the case of ICCO, DGIS has throughout the years spent an increasing part of its India budget on activities related to poverty alleviation. The policies of both organisations, however, are formulated in such a way that they leave plenty of room for manoeuvre.

It took quite some time before the two donor agencies started to take policy development concerning India more seriously. DGIS floated its first policy document specifically for this country only in the second half of the 1980s. The India policy documents, ICCO had drawn up in the late 1970s and early 1980s, were mostly confirmations of existing practice, and it was not before the 1990s that the India desk came up with a more thoroughly elaborated country-specific policy for the future. It was not only with regard to policy development that ICCO fell somewhat behind DGIS, the same goes for its attention to the environment, women and other sector-related policies.

On the level of actual aid there is even more similarity between the two donor agencies. To start with, for both ICCO and DGIS the room for manoeuvre is limited. Although caused by different circumstances (in the latter case the policy of the Indian government and in the former it was a result of a lack of sound and thorough criteria for selection and monitoring capacity) the effect is the same. In most cases there was limited leeway to direct the projects they supported. This certainly applies to a number of issues both DGIS and ICCO consider of major importance for poverty alleviation: participation, organisation and awareness-raising. These issues represent the emphasis of both agencies on what could be called the political dimension of poverty. In the majority of projects supported by DGIS and ICCO this political dimension was seriously overlooked. In essence, this means that in practice participation was often used as a 'co-opting practice, to mobilize local labour and reduce costs' (Chambers, 1995: 30). Often the donors did not succeed in moving beyond a traditional target group approach and the rhetoric of empowerment proved to be of little substance in the implementation phase. In other projects, however, both donors did progress beyond these 'co-opting practices'.

All in all, it can only be concluded from the above that DGIS and ICCO are both as effective (or as ineffective) in reaching the poor. For the poor in India it thus makes no difference through which channel 'their' projects are financed, it is the same 'difference' (Schulpen, 1997).

NOTE

1. Chapter 2 provides more detailed information on ICCO's India policy.

PART - III

PARTNERSHIP BETWEEN NORTH AND SOUTH

4

ISSUES OF PARTNERSHIP

— Fons van der Velden

A Partnership Consultation on Participatory Process was held in Calcutta, India in 1996. In the invitation it was stated that working with the people 'demands frequent and close monitoring from different angles and quarters to ensure that "we" are in the right direction. Here "we" would include the people, village workers, donor and receiver NGOs (in the traditional relationship) ...'. 'We' not automatically implies that the concerned partners relate to each other on an equal basis. In this sense partnership between non-governmental development organisations (NGDOs) from the North and the South has certainly not been unproblematic over the years. The question is what would be the right direction in order to reach more equal and sustainable relationships. One might also question whether truly equal relationships between Northern and Southern NGDOs are possible at all.

International development cooperation

Relations between Northern and Southern NGDOs take place in the broader context of international development cooperation. There are several underlying reasons for providing international development assistance. The first is what Riddell calls 'the moral case for aid': an ethical/humanitarian consideration based, not only but quite often, on a Christian tradition (Riddell, 1987, especially Part I). Other motivating factors are of political/strategic and/or economic/commercial nature (see also Chapter 1). In view of recent developments, environmental concerns and the issue of refugees may be mentioned as motivating factors for foreign aid as well (Hoebink, 1997).

In general, international development cooperation stems from the internal policy of aid-providing countries. Hence, most of bilateral aid is based on economic/commercial considerations, whereas development-related activities of most multilateral organisations relate to political and strategic interests. Structural adjustment programmes (and for that matter the debt crisis) play a major role in the imposition of the neo-liberal development model, especially in sub-Saharan Africa.

The situation is more complex, however. There are vast differences between countries and international agencies, and situations differ from place to place. Furthermore, the present rate of globalisation leads to a fast expansion of political systems and cultures under pressure, and to the world as a global village on the one side and fragmented globalism on the other (Petras, 1993; Hamelink, 1993). There are growing economic imbalances between the North and the South and between different social groups within countries. Our societies are more and more characterised by stark disparities between a privileged rich elite and disenfranchised non-citizens who are not invited to the global system.

Within worldwide international relations international development cooperation in general plays only a marginal role. Despite a substantial growth and recognition during the last decades, this is especially the case with regard to private development cooperation. Southern NGDOs have in general contributed significantly to the delivery of social services such as healthcare and education, development and poverty alleviation programmes at micro level, and less to the broader issues of promoting justice or for that matter emancipation of the people.

The midlife crisis of Northern NGDOs

In spite of the fact that a number of Northern NGDOs depend strongly on national governments or international establishments (mainly the European Union), they command an appreciable autonomy (see Chapter 1 and 8). Especially those institutions with charity and/or Church funds (for example Brot für die Welt, Misereor, Terre des Hommes, Foster Parents/Plan International, Christian Aid) are relatively autonomous.[1] This relative independence may lead to increased room for manoeuvre more or less independently from the state, and, among other things, to better opportunities to achieve qualitative changes in their relationships with counterpart organisations in the South.

Through their contribution Northern NGDOs have enabled many organisations in the South to render important services to poor and marginalised people. At the same time, however, indications are that the NGDO sector finds itself in a midlife crisis.[2] It has not managed to deal with a number of interrelated issues:

- The concept of development, and related policies and approaches of Northern NGDOs are closely linked to the historical and cultural context of the North. The 'development paradigm is a direct emanation from the modern Western pattern of thought and action' (Van Nieuwenhuijze, 1984: 16), and is rooted in a deep belief in the supremacy of the people in the North.
- A related issue is the new development syndrome. NGDOs from the North and the South have very often not succeeded in working together as equal partners. Moreover, Northern NGDOs tend to get involved more and more in the internal affairs of their Southern counterparts. Conditionality is increasing also in the NGDO sector.[3]
- One might question the core-business of Northern NGDOs. Should financing of activities still be the most important activity in view of the globalisation and the rapid 'export' of the neo-

liberal development model, the marginal importance of foreign aid, the relative unimportance of private development cooperation, and the overall limited effect of the activities? Would it not be more appropriate to devote more serious and systematic attention to policy and advocacy and educational activities in the home countries of Northern NGDOs?[4]

- The rather limited institutional learning capacity of Northern NGDOs. The resource situation in, for instance, the Netherlands for such organisations as now Cordaid, ICCO, Hivos and Novib, and also organisations active on the charity market, is still improving, and state funding as an entitlement is deeply entrenched. This may lead to a disproportionately contented attitude. Moreover, despite political pressure to show 'value for money', the attitude and mechanisms to learn from the programmes implemented by their counterpart organisations leave much to be desired.
- Last but not least, a growing number of studies indicate that the effectiveness of development cooperation is generally more limited than suggested in official documents of Northern NGDOs.

Relationship between Northern and Southern NGDOs: rhetoric and reality

Many definitions of partnership can be given for donors whose motivation stems from generous impulses of human solidarity. In his book *Not Angles but Agencies* (1995: 9-10) Michael Taylor, former director of Christian Aid, provides an adequate description of the sharing of resources approach of the World Council of Churches (WCC) that became dominant after the Nairobi Assembly in 1975:

> 'The ecumenical sharing of resources was designed to supersede the more traditional ways of giving and receiving resources typified by the project list. Its essential features are three. First, sharing was to be more equal. All would

> be givers and all would be receivers. (…) The old donor mentality was to go. Second, resources were to be understood not only as material, but were to include spiritual, theological and cultural resources, as well as personnel. Third, more people were to have a chance to make decisions or to have at least a share in making them'.

The WCC approach has substantially influenced the policy of such ecumenical organisations as Brot für die Welt, Christian Aid, EZE and ICCO. The donor-recipient relationship is inevitably awkward as the relationship is founded on inequality, which in turn reflects the world's economic system of which ethical/humanitarian-based international development cooperation by private institutions is only a small part. In reality it therefore has not been easy to achieve a working relationship between partners of the North and the South as described by WCC. As Michael Taylor (1995: 95) states:

> 'But along with these dreams come repeated confessions that the dreams have not been fulfilled: that the issue of power has not been confronted; that partnership remains an empty slogan; that words do not match deeds; that despite all the fine proposals the actual dynamics between North and South, funding agencies and receiving "partners" remain much the same; that financial considerations all too easily dominate round table discussions to make shared decisions'.

Many others have reached the same conclusion. A very interesting analysis of the question how funding agencies deal with power, moral issues and cultural differences in the relationship with partner organisation comes from ICCO's former head of the Asia Department and policy advisor for Africa Biem Lap. He concludes that due to the difference in power between providers and receivers partnership, defined in terms of equality and mutuality, is an illusion, a counterproductive myth that harms the relationship between Northern and Southern NGDOs (Lap, 1997). Based on a survey among ICCO-supported organisations in India (over 200 respondents) Lau Schulpen concludes that with regard to partnership ICCO itself has not in all cases complied with the basic requirements: transparency with regard to objectives, organisational structure, problems with regard to implementation and the internal decision-making with regard to the relationship. This opinion is shared by part of the NGDOs which participated in the survey (Schulpen, 1997).

Unequal relationships between Northern and Southern NGDOs are neither restricted to ecumenical donors nor to India. At the Conference Mutuality in South – North Cooperation (held in the Netherlands in 1995), which was attended by representatives from African, Asian, Latin American and European NGDOs, case studies were presented on collaboration between Northern and Southern NGDOs. At the end of the conference, the attendants concluded that 'the present system is rotten' and needs to be revised urgently (Dutch Association for Culture and Development, 1996: Annex 4).

Many other examples and cases could be mentioned.[5] Despite all good intentions, Northern interaction with Southern NGDOs is little more than a patron-client relationship. On paper mutual trust, respect, transparency and equality are emphasised and efforts are made to construct a degree of reciprocity in decision-making, evaluation and matters of accountability. There is abundance evidence, however, that it not always works out this way: there is a large gap between rhetoric and reality.

NGDOs have shown little ability to establish equitable relations, i.e. partnership, with each other. The question is: what went wrong? Michael Taylor (1995: 97) underlined that it is not very realistic to expect that an alternative and qualitative different relationship between parties from the North and the South will be possible, even if they meet on the basis of ethical or humanitarian grounds. The circumstances in which the Church, and for that matter the NGDO community in the North and South, try to reform themselves – in this case with regard to imbalances of power and resources in the world – amount to overwhelming odds.

Finally, Alan Fowler (1996) has identified a number of factors that stood in the way, including common factors, factors to be attributed to Northern NGDOs, factors to be attributed to Southern NGDOs, and interaction factors:

Common factors

- An incorrect, ideological conditioned, assumption that partnership involves the totality of an organisation rather than selected parts of it.
- Belated attention by North and South to the organisational dimensions of partnership.

Northern factors

- Inability of Northern NGDOs not to behave in a paternalistic manner when 'holding the purse strings'.
- In-built bias and over-valuing of Northern NGDOs' development approaches and policies.
- Insufficient, sensitive, experience and attitudinal problems from the part of Northern NGDO staff.
- There is a fundamental Northern NGDO anxiety about loss of control and reduced role which a truly empowered partner would bring.
- Until recently, insufficient public pressure on Northern NGDOs to demonstrate their performance and hence become truly dependent on partners' achievements for domestic legitimacy.

Southern factors

- The assumption that showing solidarity is a fair substitute for being effective and demonstrating performance.
- Organisational weakness and capacity limitations at the side of Southern NGDOs.
- Insufficient valuing of self-criticism and time for reflection on practice as basis for learning.
- Insufficient attention and priority to mobilising other than Northern NGDO resources from the outset.

Interaction factors

- The Northern NGDO is generally less transparent than the Southern, which disempowers.
- Discontinuity in the levels of interaction and discourse between project staff of Northern NGDOs and their counterparts in the South, leading to no in-built opportunity for dialogue between like and like in terms of position and power. Moreover, Northern desk officers are often quite junior, transient and less experienced than Southern NGDO staff, which leads to a number of problems (among others gate-keeping behaviour).
- Perpetual insecurity within Southern NGDOs that funds will be cut off, leading to a behaviour linked with this feeling.
- Insufficient attention to assess if organisational pre-conditions for partnership are in place, leading to miscommunication, frustration and disappointment.

What is to be done?

Imbalances in the relationship between private development organisations from the North and the South should be analysed within the broader framework of global interdependence which is based on neo-liberal policies, and take into account the midlife crisis of Northern NGDOs.[6]

It will not be easy to find adequate and sustainable solutions as the management and staff of many NGDOs in the North have not yet diagnosed the core of their problems, the depth of the crisis, properly. In their response crisis management is prevalent. The mainly managerial solutions, that have been proposed to solve the major issues, do not improve the work and the relationship between Northern and Southern NGDOs dramatically.

In the attitude of (representatives) of Northern NGDOs with regard to unequal relationships with Southern NGDOs three types of defence mechanisms can be observed.[7] Firstly, there is blame. Project holders in the South lack conceptual clarity, are rather secretive, lack proper management skills, do not act in a transparent and accountable manner, and do not understand. Distance is a second defence mechanism. Avoiding intense (direct) contacts and investing time to sit and discuss, prevent staff members of Northern NGDOs from the embarrassment of facing discordant views and facts. The third defence mechanism is denial of the unequal relationships and its complexities. The frequency and intensity with which NGDOs from the North defend themselves by blame, distance and denial reflects the depth of the threat by those who challenge them. To change this situation, (representatives of) Northern agencies should be more open for feedback from people at the 'coal front'.

However, the question remains whether partnership, as defined for instance by the World Council of Churches, is at all possible. In his paper Biem Lap concludes that 'partnership between givers and receivers in term of equality and mutuality is an illusion'. The idealistic approach of partnership and the rhetoric linked with it is counterproductive and does harm to the relationship between NGDOs from the North and the South. It is more fruitful to acknowledge the differences in power and the inequality so that steps can be taken to reduce the power of Northern NGDOs through a system of checks and balances. This system should contribute to a situation in which the power of Northern NGDOs can be controlled and the rights and duties of all parties involved in the development relationship be defined (Lap, 1997). Moreover, partnership is more likely to be a feature of a confident and effective relationship, and less likely to emerge from a process in which the South is subservient to quite often rather paternalistic behaviour of agencies in the North.

It could also be questioned whether onc should even try to achieve balanced and equal relationships between Northern and Southern NGDOs. If partnership between agencies from the North and the South would no longer be on the agenda, this certainly has dramatic consequences. There is a good chance that Northern NGDOs would indulge in the arrogance of power, and no longer feel the need to reflect upon the dominant paradigm of development.

Their approach could continue to be concealed in the rhetoric of concern about the plight of the poorest of the poor. A continued debate on the possibilities and desirability of partnership may contribute to the desired cultural somersault with agencies in the West and open the way for an approach which may lead to a modest change in the present practices.[8]

NOTES

1. The analysis of James Petras (1996) that foreign-funded NGDOs are just there for the promotion of the neo-liberal policy 'from below' does not do justice to the actual situation in Asia, Africa and Latin America where a number of NGDOs strongly campaign against the dominant development strategy.
2. See also Smillie (1995) and Sogge (1996).
3. The director of the Delhi-based NGDO Dastkar, Pramada Menon, in an interview states that this phenomenon is also not unfamiliar with Indian funding agencies (Huy, 1995).
4. The fact that funding agencies in the Netherlands repeatedly request their constituency to campaign for an increase in funds and not for political issues is a matter of serious concern in this respect.
5. See for instance Smillie (1995: Chapter X)
6. As has been done in a booklet by Edith Sizoo (1993): a biased – too personalised approach – might not be very helpful. Sufficient attention should be given to the political and institutional context.
7. Robert Chambers (1985) has documented how development professionals defend their 'last thinking'.
8. I thank Biem Lap for his contribution to this last concluding paragraph.

5

PARTNERSHIP IN PRACTICE :
An Analysis of the Relationship between Donor and Receiver

— *Lau Schulpen*

In July 1998, representatives of Eastern and Southern Africa NGDOs adopted the Harare Declaration on Development Relationships in which they expressed their dissatisfaction with the existing relationships between Southern and Northern NGDOs. Next to a call for Southern NGDOs to take control of the development agenda in their own countries, the Declaration calls upon Northern NGDOs to work more sincerely towards greater openness about policies, structures, functions and funding to include Southern partners in the development of their policies, structures and procedures, and to design, in cooperation with their Southern partners, appropriate strategies for organisational sustainability of these Southern NGDOs. The Declaration promotes a mature relationship with mutual transparency and accountability as cornerstones.

Using the relationship between the Dutch co-financing organisation ICCO and its Indian counterparts as a case in point, this chapter discusses partnership between Northern and Southern NGDOs with transparency as a key issue.

The donor-receiver relation

The aid - donor and aid - receiver relationship has always been difficult, if only because of the fact that one has the funds the other needs. This particularly applies to those donor NGDOs, such as ICCO, which prefer to speak about partnership with their counterparts in Third World countries rather than about aid relationship. Partnership implies a specific kind of relationship in which the 'partners' are acting on an equal footing. It implies or requires a common goal and the need to achieve this goal together, and practical measures to bring about this partnership, including discussion and exchange of ideas, mutual interest in each others organisation, means and objectives, the possibility of mutually influencing, openness, transparency and trust. Partnership, therefore, demands an interaction transcending the mere exchange of financial means from one party to the other.

Theoretically, hardly anybody will object to true partnership, particularly between NGDOs. In reality, however, matters can be quite different. For donor NGDOs it proves to be difficult to institutionalise measures that work towards partnership with their Southern counterparts. Southern NGDOs are more concerned about funding than such issues as discussion and exchange of ideas. The increase in Northern funding of Southern NGDOs in the last decade has created a new dependency. In many instances Southern NGDOs cannot finance their activities or keep their staff employed without a continuous flow of funds from the North.

ICCO in India

ICCO is one of the biggest Dutch private donor agencies and one of the so-called co-financing organisations which receive (part of) their funds from the Dutch Ministry of Development Cooperation.[1] ICCO started its activities in India in 1971. The separate India desk, that was established in 1976, remained one of the most important units in the organisation upto the mid-1990s when it was incorporated into the South Asia desk. The India desk was the biggest department with regard to applications, financial turnover and staff membership and served as a kind of guinea pig for the development of certain policy aspects. In India, for example, the

Protestant ICCO for the first time financed secular NGDOs. Whereas in the 1970s the majority of ICCO's counterparts in India were Christian, this changed gradually to one-third being secular in the early 1990s (see also Chapter 2). On other fronts (visitations, programme financing), the India desk was trend setting as well.

Two facts stand out in the policy of the India desk[2] between 1976 and 1993. First, the general objectives, although sometimes captured in different terms, remained the same: poverty alleviation with basic needs, economic development and political struggle as its components. The India desk strongly focused on political struggle. As it was realised that this political focus was largely out of the reach of most of its counterparts, an integrated approach to development was adopted. The typical 1970s and 1980s idiom of this approach (i.e., people's participation, structural changes, economic development, education, awareness-raising and organisation) was replaced by the concept of empowerment in the 1990s. The policy of the India desk was on average in line with the overall policy of ICCO (and other MFOs).

Second, in the course of the same period ICCO's India policy was refined, resulting in clearer specifications. At the beginning policies were defined in rather vague terms and mainly directed at the expansion of the project portfolio. It was only in the second half of the 1980s that the India desk took policy development more seriously. Particularly in the early 1990s, an increasing number of issues were qualified as priorities, policies or points of special interest and more strictly formulated. This stricter formulation led to a clearer concentration policy as well as to the question how to put these priorities in practice.

Between 1971-1993 ICCO funded 958 projects in India, which were implemented by 267 different NGDOs.[3] Although the India desk sanctioned projects in almost every state in India, there was (and is) a strong concentration in only a few states: Andhra Pradesh, Maharashtra, Tamil Nadu and West Bengal. Most of the projects were community development projects (so-called integrated projects) targeting the poor in general. In less than half of the projects, the target group was specified, ranging from rag pickers to tenants.

Partnership: an empty slogan?

As mentioned before, the India desk was also a nursery for policy development. It tried (in vain, as turned out later) to make the principle of sharing of power operational. This principle, from which the concept of partnership has been derived, was discussed for the first time by the ecumenical movement in the 1970s (ICCO, 1977: 16). In a 1980 policy paper, the India desk opted for the creation of an informal consultative group of Indian counterparts which could discuss its policy and assist (and evaluate) the staff members of ICCO. It was even considered to give this group a big say in the sanctioning of projects and programmes. As such, the idea of this consultative group came close to some of the central issues raised in the Harare Declaration on Development Relationships: dialogue, inclusion of Southern NGDOs in the development of policies, structures and procedures, and accountability.

In a new policy paper a few years later, this consultative group had disappeared, however. The India desk simply stated that it did not see the advantages of a further transfer (i.e. decentralisation). A number of different transfer initiatives had already been developed (ranging from rotating funds, guarantees for long-term project or programme support, and institutional support for policy consultations, seminars and advice with regard to funding). Transfer and decentralisation mainly referred to programme and organisation financing (where ICCO was not informed about the activities and budget in detail) and to advisory services of Indian consultancy agencies. More important, however, was the negative response of the Indian counterparts. They generally did not welcome the idea of project approval by Indian organisations. In addition, ICCO argued that, for reasons of accountability, direct lines with implementing organisations of funded projects were required (ICCO, 1984: 30-32).

As appears from a survey conducted in 1992-1993 among ICCO-supported NGDOs (Schulpen, 1994), not all Indian counterparts appreciated the manner in which ICCO had given substance to some of the central issues of partnership after the debacle of the consultative group in the early 1980s. ICCO was severely criticised for unilaterally decided reductions in the proposed budgets and for the attitude of ICCO staff when visiting counterparts in India, for instance the commitments made by staff members during visits and discussions which were not upheld at a later stage, frequent reshuffling of staff members in key positions, crudeness, fleeting visits. One organisation even accused the ICCO staff of being 'immature to reality'. Some of the other major points of critique can be classified as 'poor communication'. A substantial number of NGDOs felt that ICCO takes too long to respond to proposals, letters, questions and problems. Others complained that ICCO hardly gave follow-up to progress and evaluation reports. Particularly the latter point is serious, if only because these reports are requested by ICCO and therefore deserve the best of attention of the responsible staff member. The 'poor communication' type of critique was confirmed by the India desk in its 1993 policy paper which stated that the number of contacts with counterpart organisations in India should be reduced in order to achieve a manageable package of projects that can be monitored in a satisfactory way.

In the period 1989-1992 ICCO terminated the financial relationship with some 100 counterparts in India. A spring cleaning on such a scale was unprecedented and in some cases led to substantial problems with the counterparts (see below). At the same time this exercise provides an excellent opportunity to investigate the way in which ICCO put into practice one of the central issues of partnership: transparency. The following sources were consulted for reasons given by ICCO for terminating the relationship with a specific counterpart : 1) the India policy document for the period 1993-1995; 2) internal documents mentioning the reasons for termination of the relationship with a particular NGDO; 3) the letter to inform counterparts of the decision to terminate the relationship;

and 4) the reasons given by the concerned NGDO in the survey. From combining and comparing these sources the following picture emerges.

Essentially, it can be stated that the relationship with the (majority of) NGDOs was ended because of ICCO's decision to reduce the number of contracts (i.e. for ICCO internal reasons). Of course, it is not that simple. Reasons for terminating the (financial) relationship with Indian counterparts can be divided in ICCO-specific and NGDO-specific reasons. ICCO-specific reasons refer to 'changes in the policy of ICCO' and include regional priorities, 'demands' with regard to a bigger share of domestic sources in the financing of activities of ICCO counterparts, and the strategy to reduce the number of contacts in order to create a manageable and qualitatively acceptable project programme and to pay more attention to the assessment of the objectives and the proposed activities of NGDOs, the project implementation capacity and evaluation of the impact of completed projects and programmes by, for example, Indian consultancy organisations. In practice, particularly the regional priorities were used by ICCO as an argument for the termination of the relationship with NGDOs in India (see table 5.1).

'Other reasons' did play an important role as general policy guidelines but not as a justification for terminating a specific relationship. That ICCO decided to reduce the number of contracts in India is in itself not a reason applicable to a specific NGDO, but the motivation why this whole exercise was set in motion in the first place. The same applies to the increasing emphasis on better assessment of the impact of the activities of the NGDOs and their implementation capacity, organisational structure and objectives.

Table 5.1 : Reasons for terminating the (financial) relationship between ICCO and NGDOs in India as mentioned in internal ICCO documents and letters to the NGDOs (N=39)

Reasons		% of NGDOs
NGDO-specific reasons		
Organisational reasons	Internal functioning in general doubtful	41.0
	2nd-Line staff not developed	30.8
	Transparency NGDO (general/specific items)	53.9
	No clear vision-cum-policy	28.2
	Lack of checks and balances	17.9
	Weak financial planning	17.9
	Weak planning/monitoring/evaluation mechanisms	15.4
	Leadership 'underdeveloped'-cum-weak	17.9
	Insufficient number of women in staff	2.6
Implementation reasons	Impact and quality of work doubted	56.4
	Service-delivery approach	15.4
	Participation insufficient	23.1
	Group process insufficient facilitated/stimulated	12.8
	Traditional scope women programme	5.1
	Too many activities and/or fragmented	15.4
	Self-reliance target group not stimulated	15.4
	Poor follow-up on activities	2.6
Other reasons	Hardly/no or negative response to evaluation	23.1
	Mobilisation other resources	2.6
	More donors (or other funds) available	10.3
	Serious differences of opinion with ICCO	20.5
	NGDO is replacing government	5.1
	Attitude NGDO creates problems with government	2.6
	Slow rate of expenditure	2.6
	No follow-up proposal submitted	5.1
ICCO-specific reasons		
	Financial position of ICCO	10.3
	Regional policy	30.8
	General policy to reduce number of NGDOs	7.7
	Inadequate 'treatment' by ICCO	12.8

Source : ICCO project documents

For each termination specific arguments were given. The reasons mentioned in the internal documents and the letters to the NGDOs reveal that NGDO-specific reasons dominate over ICCO-specific reasons. The latter were mentioned in only 12 of the 39 cases, whereas in all cases NGDO-specific reasons were mentioned. It seems, therefore, justified to state that NGDO-specific reasons played a major role in ICCO's decision to terminate the relationship. The NGDO-specific reasons can be divided into three categories: organisation, implementation and 'other reasons'. Organisational reasons include problems with second-line staff, transparency, financial management, lack of checks and balances, development vision and reporting. Implementation reasons refer to the activities of the NGDO, their impact and the (implementation) strategy. It will be clear that the different categories of reasons are closely related and often reinforce each other. For instance, in cases where the NGDO shows no clear vision, the impact and quality of the work in the 'field' is often questioned as well. An NGDO with weak second-line staff in many cases lacks internal checks and balances. A service-oriented approach often goes hand in hand with insufficient participation of the target group or insufficient facilitating and strengthening of group processes in the villages. The fact that most NGDOs 'score' on more than one reason underlines this interrelationship.

From the letters and internal documents it appears that lack of transparency, either through (financial and narrative) reporting to ICCO or through other 'items' (letters, visits), is the most frequently mentioned NGDO-specific reason. A good second position is taken by the 'non-development of second-line staff' in the implementing organisations. Third comes the lack of a clear vision-cum-policy with regard to, for example, the implementation of activities, selection of target group and activities, and strategy to reach goals and objectives. This reason is of special interest as it suggests that ICCO, or the India desk, does have a clear vision-cum-policy on these points. Remarkably, these 'organisational reasons' are mentioned in all 39 cases surveyed.

The same does not apply to the implementation reasons. For twelve out of the 39 NGDOs, no implementation reasons were mentioned in the documents and letters. Linked to the fact that in some of these twelve cases the impact and quality of the activities of the specific NGDO were assessed positively, this leads to the conclusion that in ICCO's 'withdrawal strategy' organisational reasons are more important. The implementation reasons for the remaining 27 NGDOs can be divided into one general reason (i.e. impact and quality of work doubted) and eight more specific reasons of which insufficient participation, fragmentation of activities and a service-delivery approach are the most important ones. The reasons related to the Indian government in the category 'other reasons' seem somewhat strange considering the fact that many NGDOs in India (and elsewhere) create, through awareness-raising and organisation of the poor, 'political problems' to the more powerful in society, including (representatives of) the government. At what point NGDOs crossed the line of acceptable and non-acceptable 'struggle' did not become clear from this sample.

Together, the NGDO-specific reasons provide the picture of the ideal ICCO counterpart. Such an NGDO would be organisationally well-developed, have checks and balances secured by an independent board, have a strong but not dominating leadership and a second-line staff which is capable of acting independently and influencing policy and vision of the organisation. The policy-cum-strategy of the organisation would appear from (preferably quantifiable) objectives and goals, while the means of achieving these goals would be clear for all concerned. In its activities the NGDO would strive to self-reliance of the target group (thus making itself redundant) by awareness-raising, facilitating popular participation and setting up of strong community organisations capable of giving direction to their own development and avoiding the trap of service-delivery. Furthermore, the NGDO would be innovative in its activities and approach, and have the flexibility to adjust to different and changing situations. It would therefore adequately assess the (political, social and economic) situation in the working area and develop monitoring and evaluation mechanisms in order to be able to respond to failures and learn from experiences. The ideal NGDO would further diversify its financial sources, make the most of local sources, either from the target group or the government, be open to critique and frank about developments and problems to the (foreign) donors. Of course, it should be kept in mind that NGDOs which do not fully comply with this 'utopian sketch', will not, by definition, be excluded from ICCO support. The practice of ICCO's withdrawal strategy, however, suggests that particularly NGDOs which score low on organisational criteria are more vulnerable when it comes to continuation of ICCO support.

From the reasons given by NGDOs themselves for the termination of the (financial) relationship, it appears that for many organisations differences of opinion with regard to either vision and/or the implementation capacity are central. Most NGDOs, however, blame ICCO's change in policy. This change then refers to either: 1) the 1992 state concentration exercise which had been used before to set aside counterparts; 2) the shift from assessment of proposed activities to assessment of effects in the implementation phase; and/or 3) the financial situation of ICCO which prompted the termination exercise in the first place. Both actors thus attribute the termination of the financial relationship to each other, while they rarely search their own hearts. One of the NGDOs even accused ICCO of a 'dictatorial nature of dealing' with its partners in India (Schulpen, 1994).

The latter, of course, is of major interest when looking at partnership. Some of the reasons mentioned in internal documents and letters announcing the termination of the (financial) relationship with Indian counterparts are closely linked to central issues in partnership, for instance, the 'serious differences of opinion' and in particular to the lack of transparency of the NGDO. This raises the question whether ICCO itself is (sufficiently) transparent towards its counterparts. A comparison of the reasons as presented in the internal documents with those communicated to the concerned

NGDO shows that there are major differences. In general, the internal documents of ICCO are far more precise and to the point with regard to the critique on the NGDO. Whereas in letters to the NGDO it is often stated that ICCO doubts the quality and impact of the work of the NGDO, the internal documents reveal in more detail what is really meant by this. One of the NGDOs, for example, was told that an analysis of ten years of cooperation had shown that the impact, in relationship to the funds available, had been very limited. In the internal documents, ICCO mentions weak financial planning, poor internal organisation and a negative reaction to an evaluation report by the NGDO as additional reasons. Another ICCO counterpart was informed that it paid insufficient attention to the development of second-line staff. The internal documents also mention that the organisation was dominated by its director.

Although it is understandable that critique directed particularly at specific persons in an organisation is not easily expressed in an official letter of resignation and that cultural differences have to be taken into account, the substantial differences between internal reports and letters are a violation of the very meaning of partnership. That in some cases the letter of resignation was one of the first communications in years between ICCO and the concerned NGDO makes matters only worse. A substantial number of the counterparts with which ICCO broke off the relationship in the early 1990s had been supported for a long time. It took ICCO a couple of years to actually terminate the relationship with a major part of its counterparts in India. That it took so long was, however, not so much the outcome of a deliberate policy in which ICCO tried to rescue as many of its counterparts as possible. It was mainly the outcome of a lack of clear incentives to act upon the outcome of an internal evaluation of its counterparts in India in 1988.[4] Only when the financial position of ICCO at the end of the 1980s/beginning of the 1990s forced the organisation to act, it did so, be it in an often descriptive and even concealing manner.

Concealing is perhaps an adequate term to describe the way ICCO presents itself to its counterparts. The survey clearly showed that ICCO counterparts were in a mild state of confusion about ICCO's roles. The majority of the organisations thought that, besides funding, ICCO has to play other roles in India as well as in the Netherlands. Only a small minority held a different opinion; one organisation even stated that 'ICCO is not capable of any other function'. Interestingly, the roles mentioned by the Indian counterparts were very much in line with those mentioned in a 1993 policy paper of ICCO's India desk: advocacy, the provision of information, capacity building and networking. The organisation of seminars or other meetings for feedback were also mentioned. In the Netherlands ICCO should, according to its counterparts, especially be involved in development education, lobbying and networking. It is only in the last couple of years that ICCO has indeed been more active in these fields. Nevertheless, already in 1993 just over 50 per cent of the Indian NGDOs were convinced that ICCO was already doing so for years. Obviously, there is a large gap between ICCO's actual activities apart from direct funding and the conception of a large part of ICCO's counterparts of these activities. On the other hand, almost 40 per cent of ICCO's counterparts held the opinion that the activities of ICCO were (more or less) restricted to providing funds. ICCO partly confirmed this viewpoint by stating that '... ICCO's possibilities to support its counterparts in these ways [e.g., capacity-building, networking, information provision, advocacy] are only limited'.

The importance of foreign funding

The subscribed innovative and flexible approach of NGDOs and their direct contacts with the poor are in general the most important reasons given for the emergence of the non-governmental development organisation in the world of development assistance. The euphoria with regard to this sector as the 'sensible alternative' was almost infinite in the early 1980s (see also Chapter 1). Notwithstanding the fact that there was hardly anything known about the sector (let alone with regard to its efficiency or effectiveness), few restrained themselves from pushing NGDOs forward as the way to let development start where it should start: at the bottom, in the slums, the villages, i.e. with the poor. One could wonder (as some did) whether this happened because of the NGDOs' alleged ability to reach the poor. It is quite possible that this change was initiated by the disillusionment with twenty years of official development cooperation together with the realisation that 'governments can't do the job alone' and institutional and financial problems due to declining budgets in many donor countries. The NGDO mania led to substantial growth of the NGDO sector and, as appears from the survey, to a dependency of the NGDO sector on foreign funding. This dependency, however, is not entirely insurmountable.

ICCO's counterparts in India on average experienced a substantial growth in the number of people and communities covered, the number of staff, and in budget and expenditure. Between 1988-1992, the number of covered communities increased from 91 to 116, and the number of people reached from 115,000 to 202,000. Not all NGDOs expanded, however. Some stagnated or even experienced a decline in coverage. Although the same applies to the number of staff, there was an increase in absolute figures. Remarkably, in larger organisations the initial increase in staff in the late 1980s was followed by a slight decrease in the early 1990s.

Data on staff employed reveals more remarkable facts. Firstly, in spite of the average growth of the number of people and communities covered by the NGDOs, there was a sharp rise in 'office staff' and a decrease in 'field staff' in the beginning of the 1990s. Possibly the NGDOs concerned had gained more experience and therefore needed fewer people to do the field work. It is more likely, however, that the demands of the donor agency (i.e. ICCO) with regard to evaluation, policy development and administration in the 1990s prompted the NGDOs to a reshuffle between field and office staff. Secondly, the NGDOs employed a relatively high percentage of female staff (on average just over 40 per cent). Where field staff had to be reduced, especially women were dismissed.

The growth in coverage and staff required substantial financial resources. And indeed, the financial turnover of ICCO's counterparts showed an increase of nearly 70 per cent in the period 1988-1992. Although most evident in larger NGDOs, the budget of smaller organisations also raised. The increase in funds, and the major part of the NGDO funds in general, was provided by foreign donor agencies. More than half of the Indian counterparts of ICCO received their first foreign assistance within one year from the start of the organisation, while nearly one-third managed to acquire such funds within two to five years. Moreover, the fact that most of these NGDOs where established in the 1980s clearly indicates that particularly in that decade the number of NGDOs in India increased due to, among other things, the growing availability of foreign funds. The fact that organisations, which had started in the 1970s, claim to have received their first foreign assistance after five to ten years in operation further substantiates this finding.

Although the number of ICCO counterparts depending entirely on foreign funding is limited, the majority of them received more than 50 per cent of their annual budget from abroad. ICCO was by far not the only foreign donor. In the 1980s and early 1990s ICCO's (former) counterparts tapped funds from 147 different foreign donors. It mostly concerned small donor agencies, mentioned by only one of the counterparts. The more frequently mentioned donor agencies include NGDO, bilateral and multilateral donors. The most important NGDO donors were Oxfam, Christian Aid, EZE, Brot für die Welt, ICCO and Misereor. With the exception of Oxfam, these are all (German and British) Protestant donor agencies. Sweden, the Netherlands and Norway were the main bilateral donors, whereas UNICEF was by far the most important multilateral donor.

At the same time, foreign aid as percentage of the annual budget of former ICCO counterparts has decreased, meaning that domestic sources have become more important for NGDOs whose relationship with ICCO was terminated. Domestic resources include: 1) government funds; 2) contributions from the target group; 3) resources of the NGDO itself; and 4) bank loans. Especially resources of the NGDOs themselves (from commercial activities or corpus funds) are increasingly being used. Funds from the government come, although at some distance, second. In the early 1990s only a handful of (former) ICCO counterparts received more than 50 per cent of their annual income from the Indian government. Nevertheless, government funds have become more important, particularly for former ICCO counterparts. From the mid-1980s onwards, the Indian government has increasingly set aside funds for the financing of NGDO activities. Specific programmes have been set up and other programmes offer possibilities for NGDOs to tap funds. The government even created the Council for Advancement of People's Action and Rural Technology (CAPART) which particularly deals with funding activities of Indian NGDOs. Although many ICCO counterparts utilise governmental funds they are quite critical. They complain about the bureaucratic dealing of the government leading to a lot of paperwork, delays and a lack of flexibility, and about the interference of politicians in their work. Moreover, most NGDOs feel that the attitude of the central government towards the NGO sector is more positive than the attitude of the state governments, which, in turn, is more positive than that of the local government. As one of the NGDOs stated: 'the local government aims at fame, the state government aims at control, and the central government aims at getting things done through NGDOs without much control'. Bank loans are still a relatively unimportant local financial resource for NGDOs. Only a few have taken to this option. The same applies to the contribution of the target group, which is, with all the emphasis on tapping this source by foreign donors, quite surprising.

Summarising, from the survey it appears that foreign funding remains the single most important source of finance for ICCO counterparts in India. Simultaneously, it is not impossible to find alternative local resources when foreign funds dry up. Some NGDOs have been very successful in diversifying their financial resources. The Youth Charitable Organisation, active in Andhra Pradesh over the years, has managed to tap an amazing number of sources from India as well as from abroad. The Centre for Rural Development (CRD), working in the same state, has even been so successful in tapping government funds for its field activities that ICCO complained about not being able to follow its spending schedule. However, for its organisational costs CRD depends on one single source. Although the relationship with ICCO is (still) good, the CRD director slowly discovers that it would perhaps be wiser to diversify its sources for this part of the budget as well. Others have already experienced that depending on one donor (i.e. ICCO) can be disastrous.

After ten years of funding ICCO decided to phase out the funding of the Action for Integrated Rural Development Society (AIRDS) in the early 1990s. In contrast to other ICCO counterparts, this decision was preceded by a long period of deliberations between the NGDO and ICCO. In the course of this period AIRDS realised that the loss of the ICCO funding would endanger the further implementation of its programme and a frantic search for alternative funding was started. The efforts were largely unsuccessful, but finally AIRDS was contracted by the Dutch embassy for implementing the so-called software aspects (i.e., awareness-raising and organisation) in one of the Dutch drinking water projects in Andhra Pradesh. For reasons of malfunctioning the contract was dissolved after one year and this brought AIRDS back to another search for donors. Other NGDOs have experienced similar problems.

More than half of the NGDOs which in the early 1990s no longer had a financial relationship with ICCO, stated that the termination of this relationship had caused problems to the organisation. Some indicated that the target group was 'adversely affected' or that the 'image of the project holder and ICCO had suffered an irreparable damage in the project area', leading to a lost of faith among the target group. For most of these NGDOs the problems were more acute. Nearly 80 per cent of the former ICCO counterparts claimed that parts of their programme had to be cancelled. Moreover, nearly two-third had to dismiss staff members.

In general, those organisations, that had relied mainly (or entirely) on ICCO funding, experienced the biggest problems, although none of them had to be resolved. Most of the organisations were able to continue (part of) their activities because of other financial resources being available. The foreign origin of these resources, however, still endangers the survival of these NGDOs. The emphasis on a diversification of funding as expressed in ICCO policy papers seems to be justified. The same applies to the demand expressed in the Harare Declaration on Development Relationships that Northern NGDOs should 'work together with Southern NGDOs to design appropriate strategies for organisational sustainability of these' Southern partners.

Concluding remarks

If partnership implies a transparency at both sides concerning objectives, organisational structure, problems encountered in implementation and internal decision-making with regard to the relationship, then ICCO has certainly not in all cases obeyed to these basic rules. The criticism voiced by ICCO's counterparts quite often pointed to a paternalistic approach. The ICCO staff was accused of being insufficiently sensitive to the problems and functioning of its counterparts. 'In-built bias and over-valuing of Northern NGDOs' development approaches and policies' are not the only contributing factors in this respect. A 'fundamental Northern NGDO anxiety about loss of control and reduced role which a truly empowered partner would bring' (Fowler, 1996) is likely to play a role as well. Furthermore, the Indian NGDOs are not adequately informed about the different roles played by ICCO, leading to a mutual lack of understanding. That ICCO speaks of its 'partners' seems therefore to be misplaced. On the other hand, many of the counterparts conceive ICCO primarily as 'donor', as 'money provider', which 'indicates that the whole concept of partnership is rather a "Western"-made artificial idea than a living reality with both donors and recipients' (Riddell, R. and the DWT (Discerning the Way Together) reference group, 1993).

In conclusion, the relationship between Northern and Southern NGDOs is little more than a patron-client relationship, revealing a large gap between partnership rhetoric and reality (also see Van der Velden, 1996) and creating dependency on foreign funding. Although many of the Indian counterparts of ICCO have been quite inventive in finding alternative financial resources, many still run into deep problems when foreign funding stops. Of course, it should be taken into account that many of the ICCO counterparts in India were set aside because of doubts about the impact of their activities. Problems with the continuation of these activities should therefore perhaps not be regretted. In this context, however, it is more important that foreign funding remains the single most important financial resource for these NGDOs and that this inherently means that they are vulnerable to the whims and wishes of Northern donors.

NOTES

1. For more information on co-financing organisations and the Co-financing Programme of the Dutch government see Chapter 3.
2. In Chapter 2 ICCO's India policy is discussed in more detail.
3. Detailed information on these projects (geographical distribution, sectors, target groups and counterparts) is provided in Chapter 2.
4. For the outcomes of the evaluation see Chapter 2.

6

NORTHERN NGDOs : From Solidarity to Paternalism — The India Committee of the Netherlands

— Fons van der Velden

In 1992 the Indonesian government announced that it no longer wished to receive development aid from the Netherlands because of the Dutch government's interference in Indonesia's human rights policy. This decision resulted in the Netherlands quitting the IGGI (The International Aid consortium for Indonesia), which it was presiding for historical reasons (Schulte Nordholt, 1995).

This decree of the Indonesian government urges (yet again) to ponder on the perspective of development cooperation and on the relation between aid donor and recipient. In the light of, among other things, the economic growth of developing countries such as Brazil, India and Indonesia, governments, development agencies as well as so-called Third World groups in the Western world should fundamentally reflect on their role.

Ideological background Third World movement

The Third World movement in the Netherlands has included a great diversity of groups, institutes and individuals with different ideological backgrounds and opinions on (Dutch) development cooperation. Those who depart from a moral-humanitarian point of view argue for more help to Third World countries. They affiliate with United Nations declarations (for instance, the Human Rights

Declaration), and often feel a strong commitment to development issues.

As a result of the discussions about the world trade structure accompanying the second United Nations Conference on Trade and Traffic (UNCTAD II) at the end of the 1960s, the quality of (Dutch) development aid was criticised. From the so-called 'poor – rich approach' requests were made for 'more but better aid', and for 'no aid without social change'.

Subsequently, according to the 'solidarity approach' that was propagated in particular by student movements, development aid was considered basically good but should never benefit trade and industry. Development should be kept pure and not be contaminated by commerce.

Finally, in the 'anti-imperialistic approach' any type of help from the West was defined as a mere extension of foreign (imperialistic) policy. Development assistance was seen as a form of government intervention to remove impediments to the 'proper' functioning of foreign commercial activities (Miltenburg, 1978; Tijdschrift voor Anti-Imperialisme Scholing, 1971).

India Committee of the Netherlands

The above-mentioned solidarity approach has been the basis for the activities of the India Committee of the Netherlands (ICN), one of the trend-setting Dutch solidarity groups, since its inception.[1] The Committee was set-up at the time of the Emergency in India (1975-1977) by students and other people interested in India. In its periodical one could read until a few years ago: 'The India Committee of the Netherlands has as its aim to disseminate critical information on India. In this way, it attempts to encourage the Dutch public to develop more solidarity with progressive movements in India'.

From the early 1980s on, ICN has received financial support

from a special fund for activities related to awareness-raising on development issues of the Dutch Ministry for Development Cooperation. In the past, together with other India groups in the Netherlands and Belgium, large campaigns were organised against the delivery of fertilisers and trawlers to India by Dutch companies, and the export of milk powder by the European Union within the framework of Operation Flood.[2]

Conditionality

The protests against the delivery by Dutch companies of trawlers (1980-1981) and fertilisers (1982) exemplify ICN's solidarity approach. There is a certain degree of ambiguity in this approach, however. The attitude towards official bilateral aid is usually not clear and sometimes there is also a form of paternalism ('we know what is good for the Third World'). These points came to the fore in the ICN-sponsored campaign in 1987 against the delivery of milk powder by the European Community in the framework of the Indian programme Operation Flood. In this campaign, a plea was made for the termination of European dairy aid to India within two years. At the same time, it was demanded that aid given within the remaining two years should meet two basic conditions: 'an increase in the price of milk offered to dairy farmers in India', and 'no supply of dairy aid to bottle-feeding manufacturers'. Furthermore, the European Union was asked 'to see to it that money from the sale of the milk produced out of the dairy aid in India, will not be used for the Indian-Western cow crossbreeding programmes'.[3]

Two Indian scientists strongly protested against this form of conditionality (India Nieuwsbrief, 1986a). Usha Menon, for example, wrote: 'I want to make a plea against any form of conditionality.... If internal conditions are to be blamed for the failure of aid, then one can and should not expect the donor countries to change the internal structures in India.... It is irresponsible for Western countries, which are not even concerned with the fate of the poor in their own countries, to attempt to change the internal structures in India'. She continued her argument with: 'NGOs can give a big support by reducing the conditions which accompany aid to developing countries, and not by supporting more conditionalities, however well-intended they may be'.

A similar argument was put forward by Narendra Singh, who, after a visit to a meeting organised by the India Committee in the Netherlands, concluded that 'a missionary goodwill prevailed.... There was an abundant desire to do something for the poor there, but then according to the opinions which exist here and according to the decisions which are made here'. He argued against any 'reduction in the Indian right of self-determination' and stated: 'The desire to impose conditionalities on aid is completely undesirable and should unequivocally be rejected'. Some organisations in India responded critically as well. A group from Bangalore protested in a rather mocking manner against this Dutch paternalism by setting up the Netherlands Committee of India as a caricature of the India Committee of the Netherlands.

On behalf of ICN a staff member reacted to this criticism by stating that aid 'always goes hand in hand with a certain degree of conditionality.... I find the desire for aid without preconditions an undesirable condition for the delivery of aid' (India Nieuwsbrief, 1986b).

Once again

In 1990 ICN launched a big campaign under the slogan Work Against Poverty to assist landless people in India in their search for employment.[4] According to the information supplied by the Committee, the campaign was supported, among others, by trade unions, the funding agencies Novib and Hivos, environmentalist organisations and some other small organisations in the Netherlands.

In the light of the developments mentioned above it is unfortunate that, after so many discussions within and outside ICN concerning the conditionality of developmental aid, the same approach was chosen once again in the campaign Work against

Poverty: 'The general aim of this campaign is to make the 250 million Indian agricultural labourers and their families the primary beneficiaries of bilateral and European development cooperation with India'. The action pamphlet supporting the campaign mentioned as main objectives: 'Make agricultural labourers the most important target group of development aid'; and use debt conversion for employment guarantee'.

From the ICN documents it further appears that four Indian non-governmental development organisations (the Young India Project from Penukonda, SHED from Orissa, the Co-ordination Committee for Employment Guarantee Scheme from Tamil Nadu and the Zilla Vyauasaya Cooliela Union from Ananrapur) lobbied the Indian government to give more priority to employment-generating programmes. There is no evidence, however, that these organisations requested ICN to urge the Dutch government to tackle the Indian government on this issue.

Telling is the passage in a letter about this campaign (August 1992) to Indian NGDOs: 'The India Committee of the Netherlands is of the opinion that a considerable part of development aid to India should be used for (...). We are also asking your support for this campaign'. In a mailing to its members (December 1992) ICN announces that 'The ICN campaign takes off in India' (author's italics).

Compared to the 1987 campaign there is only a difference in words. Now it is written: 'India can then be asked ... to spend the aid entirely on programmes aimed at improving the position of the poorest income groups'. ICN claimed that the Dutch Minister of Development Cooperation 'is now willing to consider the allocation of aid to employment guarantee programmes' (Oonk, 1992), and 'agreed with the Indian government to investigate possible cooperation in financing employment guarantee programmes'.[5] During a discussion on development policy for the period 1992-1995 in the Permanent Commission for Development Cooperation of the Dutch government the spokeswoman of the influential

Christian Democratic Party, with the minister, made a plea for 'prioritising' Dutch aid to India.[6] Despite cosmetic changes in the presentation, the fact remains that here, with regard to the provision of development aid, a Dutch non-governmental development organisation insists on a foreign intervention in the policy of a reasonably functioning parliamentary democracy.

In the debate on the Indonesian question, Schulte Nordholt stressed that international political pressure in the wake of violation of human rights should be based on adequate analysis and an assessment of the political division of power. In his opinion, the aid relationship can only be used as an instrument to exert pressure when there is a violation of human rights 'due to the implementation of development projects with negative effects on the population' and violations 'which are used to protect the positions of power of the elite' (Schulte Nordholt, 1992).

By no stretch of imagination it can be argued that this applies to Dutch development cooperation with India. The campaign is therefore nothing but a contemporary form of well-intended paternalism, in which a Western solidarity group is trying to be more conservative in its policy than IMF or the World Bank.[7]

Furthermore, the ICN policies are incomprehensible in the light of the nature of the organisation itself. An action group ought to function as a critical monitor of its own government, the European Union and international organisations such as IMF and the World Bank, and to bring the functioning of these organisations into the open, instead of further stimulating and legitimising the conditionality of international aid. This case – as such – is a clear example of confusion about the roles of different development actors.[8]

Broader context

With regard to the broader issue which is at stake, the position of Northern and Southern NGDOs, vis-à-vis conditionality, ICN and other solidarity groups may learn some lessons from a dialogue organised by INTRAC (an Oxford-based support organisation for NGDOs) on this issue (Clayton, 1994).

The participants of the INTRAC workshop took a central feature of conditionality, the asymmetrical relationship between Northern and Southern governments, as a starting point for their discussions. Quite often Southern governments are asked or forced to adopt policies formulated by Northern governments or international agencies that are actually not pursued in the North. The structural adjustment programmes are a case in point. These programmes, which were forced upon many developing countries in the 1980s, would never have been accepted by many governments in the North. Taking into consideration the mandate and constituency of Northern NGDOs, including ICN, NGDOs need to challenge the hypocrisy and inconsistency of Western governments in the conditions they impose on development cooperation instead of providing legitimacy to this conditionality. Organisations as ICN should aim to end the North-South imbalance of power rather than discuss ways to cope with it.

Furthermore, NGDOs should not put too much emphasis on formal political processes; commercial and strategic interests might be a better priority. Northern NGDOs should also try to avoid inventing demands on behalf of the people in the South. This principle applies especially to the above-described ICN campaigns. Interventions should take place in solidarity with and in response to demands of organisations in the South rather than on their behalf.

> 'There is a real danger that the Northern NGOs are being forced to ally themselves more with donor governments and separate themselves from their Southern partners because of the new policy agenda on governance and conditionality. This is especially the case for those NGOs that are dependent on government funding sources. There is a need for Northern NGOs to take more initiative and more risks in criticising the lack of overall coherence in

> the policies of Northern governments. Advocacy and lobbying of bilateral and multilateral donors should be more central to development activities of NGOs. However, the institutional constraints and realities faced by some NGOs make it difficult for them to be so proactive without threatening their practical, grassroots activities. In addition, NGOs need to carefully consult local NGOs when formulating their strategy of advocating for reduction or cancellation of international development assistance to certain governments.
>
> There is a further need for Northern NGOs to engage with governments in lobbying multilateral organisations. International institutions, such as the World Bank, OECD, and the UN Security Council, are trying to force the governance agenda onto Southern governments, yet they themselves are undemocratic institutions with relatively low levels of accountability. Governments need to pressurise such organisations to become more accountable' (Clayton, 1994: 123-124).

Peanuts

Apart from the above-mentioned facts, there is a second reason to critically examine the ICN campaign. The importance of foreign aid has drastically decreased in the course of time. According to figures from the World Bank, the foreign aid India received over the last few years accounted for just around one per cent of its Gross National Product (in Bangladesh this was approximately ten per cent). During the last decades the total Dutch share in foreign aid to India amounted to about five per cent. In the light of these figures, the use of the power of money is not a very realistic option. The Indian Minister of Finance will not have sleepless nights when financial support from the Netherlands stops. Furthermore, the sale of illusions will not help the Dutch population to gain a better understanding of the background and problems of underdevelopment and independence.

Perhaps it would be a better idea for ICN to focus its activities on the functioning of IMF, the World Bank and GATT and restrict its 'lobbying activities' to the Dutch government, the European Union or Dutch corporations. However, as stressed by Update Collective (a group of Indian activists) in their reaction to the ICN campaign, this should be done without requesting them 'to pressurise' a sovereign state ruled by a democratically elected government. With regard to the campaign Update Collective stated: 'We are of the opinion that a few issues being dealt with in this campaign ought to be clarified and enlightened.... We wonder whether the emphasis on employment generation is only desirable'. This group also made a plea for loan waiver instead of debt conversion ('it does not solve anything') (Update Collective, 1992).

Finally, the employment guarantee can be questioned. Robert Chambers, N.C. Saxena and Tushar Shah (1989) summarised the priorities of India's poor as follows: surviving (based on a stable income and consumption), security (based on the ownership/control of land) and self-respect (based on independence and choice). The employment guarantee schemes propagated by ICN only partially fulfil these priorities. The ICN approach is what Chambers et. al. call a product of 'employment thinking'.

Would, in view of the nature of poverty in rural India, the right to the means of production such as land not be a more adequate option? On the basis of elaborate studies of rural West Bengal, Lieten states: 'Land reforms are referred to as "a past station" (Myrdal) and as "an old refrain", but it is worth the effort to ride back to the station' (Lieten, 1992: 289).

NOTES

1. For an overview of the history of ICN see Van de Waal (1987) and Beerends (1993: 259-261).
2. See also the ICN (Landelijke India Werkgroep) publications 'Blauwe revolutie' in India; miljoenen vissers bedreigd door opmars trawlers (1981); De Nederlandse kunstmest hulp/handel aan India (1982) and India als melkkoe van de EG (1985).

3. See Landelijke India Werkgroep, ibid., 1985.
4. The brochure Werk tegen Armoede; een ander ontwikkelingsbeleid voor 100 miljoen Indiase landlozen (Landelijke India Werkgroep, 1990), and the article Campagne 'Werk tegen Armoede' succesvol van start in: India Nu (1991). The author's earlier commentary on this campaign, entitled Mag het ietsje minder zijn? Een andere visie op de LIW-campagne 'Werk tegen armoede' was published in India Nu (Van der Velden 1992). In his reaction Ontwikkelingshulp: geen blanco cheque; kritiek op campagne 'Werk tegen Armoede' misplaatst (Oonk, 1992), ICN staff member Gerard Oonk vividly expresses the ICN ideas on this matter.
5. These intentions had already been mentioned in the country policy document for India prepared in 1991: India – Beleidsplan voor de periode 1992-1995 (Ministerie van Buitenlandse Zaken, 1992: 31).
6. She stated: 'The cooperation in the area of agricultural development should (...) be focussed on the marginal farmers and the landless rural poor'. The minister responded: 'The Netherlands has always wanted to give more project aid, whereas India asks for programme aid' (Handelingen van de Tweede Kamer, 1992-1993, no. 6, pp. 2 & 12).
7. The following incident may be seen as a manifestation of the would-be cooptation of the ICN by the establishment. When the Dutch version of this article was published in a Dutch journal, the chairperson and a senior staff member of the ICN wrote a letter to the then employer of the author requesting to see that he 'would keep his big mouth shut' about this issue. (It did not work.)
8. See also Chapter 8.

PART - IV

NGDOS : CHALLENGES FOR THE FUTURE

7

DEMOCRATISATION AND THE ROLE OF NGDOs : Two Cases from India

— *Lau Schulpen*

It has increasingly been realised that development is about more than economics. The idea that the people concerned must have a say in the process of development is gaining ground. Two major issues in this respect are participation and democratisation. By examining the evolution of non-governmental development organisations and experiences in India, this chapter discusses the possible role of these organisations in the advancement of participation and democratisation.

The concept of development

The concept of development is often interpreted as economic development at an individual, national or international level. Growth of the National Product, export promotion, industrial development are supposed to be indicators of economic development. Development, however, involves much more than just economics. It also concerns human development, through, for example, education, access to safe drinking water, human rights and political participation. Especially after the 1980s, the structural adjustment decade, professionals have paid more attention to the concept of development. Although different actors in the development scene use different words and definitions, they increasingly agree that development in the first place refers to the development of human resources. UNDP states that 'the basic objective of development is to create an enabling environment for people to enjoy long, healthy and creative lives' (UNDP, 1990: 9). The Dutch Ministry for Development Cooperation (DGIS) defines development in terms of 'development by, for and of the people' (Ministerie van Buitenlandse Zaken, 1991: 159).

DGIS further regards poverty alleviation as the prime objective of development. This view is shared by John Clark who, in his book on the role of voluntary organisations in development, remarks: 'the principal objective of development must be the eradication of poverty and its underlying causes' (Clark, 1991: 19). Although this does not imply that the terms development and poverty alleviation are interchangeable, there is a clear indication that they are at least related. Development cannot be seen as a purely economic process, nor can poverty alleviation. The end of the 1980s showed a reconfirmation and an elaboration of the three dimensions of poverty (or for that matter poverty alleviation and development): social, economic and political dimensions. The social dimension refers to 'inadequate access to the basic amenities necessary for a dignified existence', the economic dimension to 'unequal distribution of resources ... and inadequate exploitation of these resources', and the political dimension to 'little or no access to the decision-making process' and human rights (Ministerie van Buitenlandse Zaken, 1991: 145). In poverty alleviation these dimensions are inseparable and should all be taken into account.

The view 'food first, then ethics' still has its merits in the practice of the development process. The linkage, however, between the three above-mentioned dimensions of poverty, poverty alleviation and development makes this view questionable in the long run. The political dimension is increasingly considered decisive for sustainable economic and social development. In other words: 'Democracy and classical human rights are ... essential preconditions for sustainable and evenly distributed development' (Ministerie van Buitenlandse Zaken, 1991: 57). This is not to say that economic and social development (in the sense of income, employment and fulfilment of basic needs) are unimportant. With respect to Latin America Schuurman (1992a: 40-63), for instance, states that democratisation and economic development are linked to each other and that a democratic order is an essential (but not necessarily sufficient) precondition for a structural improvement in the position of the underprivileged.

Following the above, development is defined here as 'a process of change that enables people to take charge of their own destinies and realise their full potential. It requires building up in the people the confidence, skills, assets and freedom necessary to achieve this goal' (Clark, 1991: 26). Such a definition clearly states that development is closely linked with the concepts of participation and democratisation which are playing an increasingly important role in the debate on development. Development, as defined above, is in last instance a political process, in which people develop the capacity to play 'a role in the economic and political choices' (Smillie & Helmich, 1994: 7) their society has to make, and are able to participate in and benefit from programmes meant for them. The terms democracy and democratisation should not be confused with their meaning in the context of Western parliamentary democracy. The term democracy is used here in its purest form, i.e. a form of government in which the people rule. In essence, democracy means that opportunities are created for people to have a say in what is happening and that they are able to participate in decisions which have an impact on their lives. The way democracy takes shape depends on the cultural, social and economic conditions of a particular society.

The concept often connected to the process of democratisation is empowerment. In the context of the political dimension of poverty/development it means that the conditions should be created for an active participation of the people in the decision-making structure of their society, at the local as well as the national level. As key actors in the field of democratisation and development/poverty alleviation, governments play an important role in this process. However, this role is currently being undermined by the worldwide phenomenon of privatisation. Inspired by former 'world leaders' like Reagan and Thatcher and the dismantling of the 'socialist system', the 1980s witnessed retreating government involvement and calls for greater involvement of the private sector in development. Captured under the term good governance, the role of the government has been reduced to creating 'a conducive social, economic and political environment in which development may take place through a mixture of public and private initiatives' (Smillie & Helmich, 1994: 7). In creating the conditions for active participation of the population in decision-making processes, people in many Third World countries are apparently left to their own devices. It is within this neo-liberal context that non-governmental development organisations (NGDOS) could play a role in creating the conditions for active participation (and a better utilisation of schemes initiated by governments) and thus initiate or accelerate processes of democratisation.

NGDOs: from relief to advocacy

As the term non-governmental development organisation only indicates that the organisation is not part of the government machinery a further refinement is necessary. Non-governmental development organisations come in many shapes and forms. In the literature a division is often made between people's organisations (in UNDP terms: democratic organisations that represent the interests of their members and are accountable to them) and NGDOS. NGDOs, as seen by UNDP, are voluntary organisations that work with, and very often on behalf of, other people and/or organisations. People's organisations and NGDOs can have very close links. The most striking difference is probably their organisational form: NGDOs frequently have 'bureaucratic hierarchies without the democratic characteristics or accountability of most people's groups' (see, for instance, UNDP,1993: 8). Other divisions are also possible. The general policy document of the Dutch co-financing organisation ICCO, for instance, distinguishes: 1) base or target group organisations; 2) intermediate organisations or NGDOs; and 3) societal organisations (ICCO, 1993a: 11). The Dutch Impact Study divides base organisations into formal organisations (for instance cooperations and trade unions) and informal organisations (groups formed in villages and wards and other grassroots organisations) (Steering Committee Impact Study, 1991: 5). In the field of development studies, activities and assistance, the term NGDO is mainly allocated to those organisations having development as an explicit goal.

In the context of this chapter NGDOs are defined as organisations, whether originating from the target group or not, which work directly or indirectly in the area of poverty alleviation (including economic, political and social development). Since this is still a broad definition it is necessary to make some more distinctions. In first instance, it is necessary to distinguish between Northern and Southern NGDOs. Although a certain overlap is possible, Northern NGDOs normally are donor NGDOs. They finance, with money from the government and/or the public, development projects and programmes in Third World countries. Many of them are also involved nationally and increasingly internationally in advocacy[1] and awareness campaigns.[2] An enormous increase in the amount of money governments made available to Northern NGDOs led to a NGDO mania in the 1980s. Donor NGDOs show a remarkable variety as to strategy, ideology and fundraising. In the Netherlands the most important donor NGDOs are the four so-called co-financing organisations: Cordaid, ICCO, Novib and Hivos. In their wake there is a whole range of organisations ranging from primary schools collecting money for a project of a local priest in an African country to the Centres for Development Cooperation aimed at awareness-raising on development issues in the Netherlands.

Organisations implementing the projects and programmes financed by Northern NGDOs are either these Northern NGDOs themselves or, more often, Southern NGDOs. Southern NGDOs are possibly even more diverse than their Northern counterparts. In India, for instance, aware, until recently supported by a consortium of donors among which Novib and ICCO, is active in five states, employs a staff of many hundreds of people and has an annual budget of millions of Dutch guilders. At the other end of the scale, there are small local NGDOs, working solely in a part of a village, and implementing a low-budget programme without any outside assistance. However, a division along these lines, or equally a division on the basis of the use of local and/or foreign funds, is less meaningful as a division on the basis of the strategy followed by the organisation.[3]

Three generations of NGDOs

In India, NGDOs (or voluntary organisations as they are usually called) are generally divided into three groups. The first group comprises welfare organisations which aim at meeting an immediate deficiency or shortage. Organisations aiming at economic and social development and characterised by income-generating programmes and a basic needs strategy form the second group. The third group, often labelled social action groups, focuses on awareness-raising and empowerment of the target group and has participation as a central theme. This division is far from static: organisations can have characteristics of each of the three groups. More recently, a fourth category of NGDOs has been distinguished: intermediate organisations. These organisations are not directly involved with the target group but provide services to other NGDOs. Because of the fact that the expertise of some of the intermediate organisations is for sale, some people feel that they should actually be seen as 'commercial companies in disguise' (UNDP, 1993: 88).

The Indian NGDO categorisation can be traced back to the NGDO categorisation by Korten in his article for World Development in 1987. Korten (1987: 145-159) distinguishes three generations of NGDOs, using 'relief and welfare', 'small-scale self-reliant local development', and 'sustainable systems development' as indicators. The first generation of non-governmental development organisations aims, as in the Indian example above, at the alleviation of direct needs. The NGDO itself is the most important actor and the target group is not or hardly involved. The 'small-scale self-reliant local development' generation emerged at the end of the 1970s and started programmes on preventive healthcare, local infrastructure and other community-oriented projects. As the emphasis was on local self-reliance and sustainability, participation of the target group in the programme became a necessity. According to Korten many of the programmes of this second generation NGDO run parallel to government programmes. The still small-scale activities of these NGDOs left no room for an analysis of the causes of inequality in a wider context. This characteristic led to the emergence of a third generation of NGDOs.

The insight that for small-scale activities to have a real impact the support of an (inter)national system is essential has resulted in increasing efforts of a growing number of NGDOs to influence policy-making on regional, national and international levels. (Inter)national advocacy has become a major concern for third generation NGDOs. The Conference on Environment in Rio de Janeiro (1992) and thc Social Summit in Copenhagen (1995) have learnt that cooperation between Northern and Southern NGDOs is an important condition for lobbying activities to be successful. On the national level NGDOs create networks to increase the pressure on the government. Many governments, both in the North and the South, appear sensitive to this kind of advocacy.

Korten's categorisation does not sufficiently take into account the fact that the majority of Southern NGDOs still belong to the first two generations of NGDOs and that within the second generation a subdivision can (and should) be made referring to the strategy of the organisations with regard to local activities. This mainly applies to the empowerment strategy of NGDOs, in which participation of the target group is a key issue. Awareness campaigns, education and organisation of the target group are for more NGDOs than ever a regular programme component. The objectives are twofold: first, to reach sustainable poverty alleviation, and, second, influence the policies of regional and national governments through a process of mental, economic, social and political strengthening of the target group

According to Thérien (1991: 263-280) four generations of NGDOs can be distinguished on the basis of their 'charitable, developmental, participatory, or globalist approaches'. It is especially in the 'participation' generation of NGDOs that the concept of empowerment plays a role.

NGDO as most privileged channel

The NGDO mania of the 1980s went hand in hand with a relative ignorance of the phenomenon itself. The notion that NGDOs were active at the local level, were better equipped to reach the poor, and that their programmes had a more substantial and sustainable impact on the target group was sufficient to award NGDOs the status of 'most privileged channel'. This notion was strengthened by general dissatisfaction with programmes of bilateral and multilateral donors and pronouncements from the NGDO sector itself. NGDOs were pushed forward as the new instruments of development cooperation that would ensure that aid reaches the intended target group: the poor. Moreover, and this is of eminent importance for the discussion here, NGDOs were seen as a pivot, as the embryo of the democratisation process. In other words, through their focus on economic, social and (in particular) political empowerment, NGDOs were supposed to carry with them the possibilities to contribute to a more equal and democratic society: the NGDO as the third power in society.

Although reaching the poor and contributing to the process of democratisation may at first instance seem quite different objectives, it is the (assumed) interrelationship between the two that makes NGDOs so interesting. In the local activities of a growing number of NGDOs, empowerment plays an increasingly important role. At the same time NGDO networks try to influence policy making and implementation at regional, national and international levels. In fact, it could be stated that NGDOs support the democratisation process in two different ways: indirectly by empowerment of the poorer segments of the population, and directly by advocacy through cooperation between NGDOs.

As a result of the renewed attention for human resources in development thinking concepts as participation, development from below, and awareness-raising were taken out of mothballs as the alternative to the structural adjustment policy of the 1980s. This policy, propagated by the World Bank and IMF with bilateral donors in their wake, was at least in one sense structural: the poor were structurally left out. It is mainly the attention for participation which makes NGDOs a perfect instrument in the eyes of policy-makers. Last but not least, NGDOs fitted into the spirit of times perfectly because of their non-governmental nature. Liberalisation and retreating governments made way for a 'de-bureaucratisation of development aid' (Schiel, 1987: 79-92).

The question that should be asked (and is increasingly being asked) is whether NGDOs, after their sudden thrust into the centre of attention, will be able to fulfil all expectations? Is the individual NGDO indeed capable of reaching the poor? do the strategies of NGDOs, which in theory are aimed at participation and empowerment, work? are NGDOs capable of influencing national and international policy? Recent studies on the local activities of ngdos, and (to a lesser extent) on their advocacy activities, indicate that time may have come to readjust the expectations.

Determinants of impact

To determine the possibilities of any NGDO to significantly contribute to development in a Third World country, three important factors should be considered: 1) the relationship with foreign donors; 2) the relationship with their own governments; and 3) the NGDOs, own organisational structure, strategy and ideology.

One of the most visible consequences of the increased attention for NGDOs is the growing amount of money transferred through

Northern NGDOs to Southern NGDOs. 'Counted at 1986 prices the development aid through NGDOs rose from $2.7 billion in 1970 to $6.4 billion in 1989' (Steering Committee Impact Study, 1991: 16). NGDOs are increasingly being funded directly by bilateral and multilateral donors (see also Schulpen, 1991: 4-6). In Andhra Pradesh (India), for instance, the Dutch Ministry of Development Cooperation has financed drinking water and sanitation projects. A third contributor to the growing funds available for the NGDO sector are governments in developing countries. In the mid-1980s the Indian Government officially recognised the 'voluntary sector' as an important channel and source for development, and consequently set aside funds for these organisations.

The enormous growth of funds has led to an expansion of the NGDO sector, both with regard to individual NGDOs and (perhaps more important) the number of ngdos (see Chapter 1). This swift growth not only has positive effects. NGDOs in general have become more dependent on foreign funds and, at the same time, the pressure on the sector has increased. Whichever way one looks at it, aid (and certainly bilateral and multilateral aid) still aims at quick results. This 'quick-result-race' proves to be counterproductive for organisations using a participatory strategy (see, for instance, UNDP, 1993: 89). Increasing dependency on foreign funds has brought with it requirements of professionalism, evaluation and reporting which many NGDOs could not meet. Lastly, the pressure on the NGDO sector further increased by the simple fact that they were suddenly presented as the alternative solution. Due to the high hopes it became almost impossible for NGDOs to confine themselves to the local level and not to pay attention to the wider context. They were supposed to spread their wings. It goes without saying that they were also expected not to forget their 'grassroots origins and links' in doing so (see, for instance, Drabek, 1987: ix). These remarks are not to suggest that such developments should be stopped but to illustrate the growing pressure on the sector to meet a variety of expectations, while the ones who express these expectations do not always realise that the NGDOs are not in all cases equipped to do so.

The second very important factor affecting the impact of both local and advocacy activities of NGDOs is their relationship with the government. It may be clear that because of the enormous differences between countries making generalisations is a tricky business. The conclusion: 'the more open and democratic a system is, the more varied and complicated a possible relationship between the state and the NGDOs' seems to be an open door. It points out, however, the complexity of making generalisations. (Steering Committee Impact Study, 1991: 17-19). The relationship between NGDOs and the state ranges from complete repression of local, private initiatives by the government to admitting NGDOs to decision-making processes. Even in the latter case, one can ask whether this happens because of the possible contribution of NGDOs or because it is seen by the government as a way to coopetate the NGDOs. In India NGDOs have been officially recognised as partners in development since the mid-1980s. As a result, more funds have been made available to the NGDOs (for example through CAPART),[4] and NGDOs have been invited to participate in consultative bodies. Although there are clear successes with regard to the influence of NGDOs on government policy (the national health policy of India has largely been derived from NGDO experiences), the state at the same time creates the possibility of keeping an eye on the sector. NGDOs have to register as an organisation, they need special permission to receive foreign funds and the government demands an annual financial report. In addition, the Indian government has also tried (in vain) to set-up a National Forum for NGDOs. While part of the sector was charmed by the idea (especially in view of the possibilities it would create for influencing national and regional government policies), another part saw no advantages at all. In their eyes the Forum was merely a mechanism to exercise greater control over the sector.

Even in countries where the national policy is in favour of the NGDOs sector (as in India), there is still the discrepancy between the official policy and the implementation of that policy by lower level and local governments and government officials. In India, a survey among 119 (former) ICCO counterparts showed that 51 per cent held the opinion that differences do exist between the attitude of central, regional and local governments towards the NGDO sector; 38 per cent regarded the central government as much more positive than the local, as opposed to only eight per cent who thought it was the other way around (see also Schulpen, 1997). Many local governments conceive NGDOs as an attack on their status and/or their possibilities to enhance their income by receiving and controlling government funds.[5] Here we come to the assumed advantages of NGDOs in reaching the poor and simultaneously contribute to a more equal and democratic society.

Participation of the target group in the developmental process, whether at a local or higher level, and activities in the field of empowerment (in social, economic and political sense) form the points of departure here. Critical questions must be raised, for example, as to whether NGDOs tend to take over tasks of the government without paying much (if any) attention to the actual participation of the target group in the whole process. With regard to NGDOs which claim to apply participatory and empowerment strategies, one can ask whether this is merely rhetoric inspired by the necessity of satisfying the donors.

The Dutch Impact Study concluded that NGDOs in general did have a participatory approach and that they succeeded in contributing to the empowerment of the target group. Quantitative evidence for this conclusion could not be given (Steering Committee Impact Study, 1991: 35). An evaluation, carried out by the Overseas Development Institute (ODI) of sixteen NGDO projects in the field of direct poverty alleviation, concluded that the formation of grassroots organisations, in general seen as an important process within the framework of participation and empowerment, in some of the cases did not surpass similar efforts in non-NGDO projects. In five out of the sixteen cases, community participation was regarded as insufficient (Riddell & Robinson, 1992: 20-21). The ODI evaluation further concluded that NGDOs do not necessarily reach the poorest of the poor, although they are more effective in this respect than the programmes of governments and bilateral and multilateral donors. UNDP laconically states in this regard: 'If government and official aid programmes usually fail to reach the poorest 20 per cent of income groups, most NGDO interventions probably miss the poorest 5-10 per cent' (UNDP, 1993: 96).

Although recent studies on NGDOs and their impact reach similar conclusions, it remains difficult to make universally valid statements on this issue because of the diversity of NGDOs and the differences in political, economic and social environment. What these studies do show is that the small scale of NGDO activities in general does not correspond with a broad, if not decisive, effect on the position of the poor, and that several factors play a role in the impact of NGDO interventions. These factors relate to the already mentioned relationship with donors and governments and to the relationship between NGDOS, the quality of their staff, their organisational structure (in particular leadership), the formulation and operationalisation of objectives and targets, and learning from experiences (see also Chapter 2).

The more studies on NGDOs are published and the experience of donors in working with NGDOs increases, the more the euphoria with regard to NGDOs diminishes. It is increasingly being realised, for example, that notwithstanding the growth of the sector the activities of NGDOs remain 'a drop in the ocean', that NGDOs also have problems in reaching the poor, that there is a great diversity within the sector, and that not all NGDOs view 'reaching a just and democratic society' as one of their most important objectives. Despite this dampened optimism, NGDOs remain an important issue in the discussion on development. There is a clear shift in thinking. In its 1993 Report UNDP recognises external and internal problems of NGDOs operating at a local level, and sees advocacy as the major strength of the sector.

Advocacy refers to the outside world and manifests itself in for instance 'development and public education work, awareness-raising, lobbying, networking, dialogue and campaigning' (Riddell and the DWT reference group, 1993: 41). Advocacy (especially at the national level) is geared to a more democratic society. If NGDOs transcend their local activities aimed at poverty alleviation in a narrow sense, they could contribute to such a democratic society. NGDOs could play a role in bringing together the government and the people by sensitising the first one on such issues as the needs, aspirations and possibilities of the people, and the latter on the functioning and the structure of the government. This could result in public accountability, in more extensive participation of the population in development programmes initiated by governments, in more interaction between the two actors, and, eventually in better mutual understanding and a higher impact of development programmes.

India: two cases

In connection to the above discussion on NGDOs and their possible role in increasing democratisation two cases from India are presented. The first refers to the activities of the Centre for Rural Development operating in Guntur District, Andhra Pradesh, since the beginning of the 1980s. The second concerns the Programme Support Unit, originally set-up within the drinking water programme in Uttar Pradesh, co-financed by the Dutch government.

Centre for Rural Development

The Centre for Rural Development (CRD) encourages members of its target group (consisting mainly of scheduled castes and tribes) to make use of government schemes. The organisation also plays an important role in the implementation of several government schemes. People are informed about different schemes available to them and learn how to apply for these schemes by themselves. CRD also acts as a selector of beneficiaries, makes sure that repayments on the loan part of government schemes are made in time, and that people optimally use the assets received through government schemes. In cooperation with CRD these activities are carried out by organisations of the target group especially created for this purpose in the villages (see also Chapter 3).

For its own activities CRD follows strict procedures: decisions with regard to activities to be undertaken, funds to be allotted and selection of beneficiaries are taken by the villagers themselves in a three-tier structure consisting of village, area and programme levels. At each of these levels representatives of the target group are elected by the villagers every two years. Although the relationship with the government is still largely restricted to CRD, the growing awareness of the target group with regard to its contacts with the government machinery and its strong involvement in village organisations has brought about a beginning of empowerment. People are now in a better position to stand for their rights independently of the implementing NGDO.

The mode of operation of CRD is not unique, but certainly also not very common. Many of the NGDOs in India confine themselves to their own programmes and only make use of government schemes on an incidental basis. It is also certainly not always the case that, when it comes to government schemes, members of the target group are in any way involved in selecting beneficiaries, in writing formal applications and in personal contacts with government officials. It is easy to underestimate as well as overestimate the role played by NGDOs in the field of creating an atmosphere of better understanding and coordination between the government machinery and 'ordinary' people. Driven by, among other factors, anger about the bribes asked by government officials, some NGDOs refuse to use government funds and, even worse, activate their target group to do the same. As a result, people have no information at all about schemes that are in principle available to them (and to which they have a right), and have not the slightest notion of how to handle applications, government officials and all other things (including bribery) that come with any interaction with the government machinery. Such a policy is counterproductive; it denies people their rights, and, above all, prevents a closer participatory interaction between the people and the government.

Programme Support Unit

One of the main reasons why the Programme Support Unit (PSU) in Uttar Pradesh attempts to establish a structure in which there is more interaction and a better understanding between governmental bodies and the villagers to enhance the opportunities for popular participation. PSU was set up in 1988 as part of the Dutch-financed drinking water programme in Uttar Pradesh. The failure of incorporating the so-called software aspects (i.e. health promotion, participation, organisation) in the government machinery responsible for the physical implementation of the drinking water and sanitation programmes underlay the decision to make a team of people from outside the project (and thus the government) responsible for this important part of the programme.

The limited staff capacity of PSU made the implementation of the software part in all villages concerned impossible. It was therefore decided to concentrate on a few selected villages, which should become model villages (or, in PSU terms: Intensive Mobilisation Villages (IMVS). These IMVS should, in turn, encourage other surrounding villages to follow their example. Although some progress has already been made, the second part of the new strategy (under the name Expanded Base of Community Participation) is, for the discussion here, more important. PSU realised that the entry point of drinking water and sanitation was in the longer run insufficient to build and sustain popular participation of the villagers. To stimulate the villagers to use and maintain the provided assets and enhance community development, other activities had to be developed. Because of PSU's limited financial and organisational means, government schemes seemed to be a logical outcome. PSU was aware of the shortcomings of these schemes: the selection of beneficiaries was not always done according to the guidelines, follow-up was often not provided, and the schemes were offered to people who took no interest in them. PSU decided to create the so-called Block Coordination Committees and District Coordination Committees in which government officials, PSU representatives and representatives of the established village organisations come together to discuss possible programmes for the separate villages in general and the villagers in particular. Through this formal structure the exchange of information between the government and to the people has been made possible and the conditions have been created for more active participation of the people in the implementation of the government schemes and more custom-made programmes. It should be mentioned, however, that it is still unclear whether the structures set up under the auspices of the PSU will indeed work out. In the context of this chapter this is not relevant. What matters is that opportunities have been created for closer contacts and coordination between the providers and the beneficiaries of the schemes, and (again, in theory) for adjustments of the schemes following discussions about the schemes between the parties involved. Such a constellation transcends the programme or project level for it also creates the opportunity for a better mutual understanding and thus for what is often referred to as good governance.

The above-described examples show that NGDOs operate on different levels. On the one side, there are NGDOs which implement programmes at the local level and make no effort towards alteration of the structure of society. On the other hand, there are NGDOs which do aim at structural changes. These changes can be local in the sense that the activities of the NGDO do not go beyond the local structure (for instance, a change in the attitude of local higher castes towards the lower castes). Structural change can also be related to the government (in spite of everything still an important actor). In this case it may be confined to the alteration of the implementation structure of government schemes in order to increase the impact of these schemes on people's lives, or go beyond this and include the search for more active interaction between government structures and people in order to create a better understanding, cooperation, accountability and participation (i.e. to create a more democratic society).

Panchayati Raj Institutions

Interestingly enough, neither of the two above-discussed NGDOs pay explicit attention to one of the most important developments in the Indian state structure: the Panchayati Raj Institutions (PRI, village councils). It could even be stated that these NGDOs create separate structures that are intended to play a role in the village life next to the Panchayats. Although this is quite common among NGDOs, there are also organisations that do pay specific attention to the (functioning of the) panchayats by, for example, training their target groups or by training panchayata members.

The implicit 'denial' of the PRI by CRD and PSU is the more interesting as PRI is considered to be a key stone to decentralisation and democratisation in India. According to Mathew (1995: 3) 'there is no other socio-political programme launched by the government in independent India which has generated as much enthusiasm and participation of the people as the panchayati raj institutions'. He immediately adds, however, that the PRIs have gone through distinctive phases and actually 'developed a tendency for imminent collapse' at the time that their potential was reaching its peak. To the three historical phases Mathew distinguishes (i.e. 1959-1964: phase of ascendancy; 1965-1969: phase of stagnation; and 1969-1977: phase of decline, followed by even further decline) a new phase can be added which officially started with the 73rd and 74th amendments to the Constitution. The constitutional and legal framework of decentralisation in India now consists of a three-tier structure of government: local, state and federal. 'At the local level, there are Panchayats at the village, block and district levels, and three grades of municipalities depending on pre-determined factors such as population, functions and the economic base' (World Bank, 2000: 53).

In 1999, there were over 215,000 village panchayats in 20 Indian states. However, according to the World Bank (2000), the new PRI structure has upto now not been entirely successful. In fact, decentralisation is far from complete and 'cracks are already beginning to surface in the evolving systems of fiscal and functional decentralization'. The capacity of the panchayats in formulating policy was rated as inadequate, whereas accountability was negligible and service delivery and revenue collection even more inadequate. It goes to show that the new PRI structure, despite its many potential positive features in the field of raising a voice for the poor and women, still has a long way to go. It simultaneously appears that these problems are partly of a legal nature (differences between states, financial decentralisation) and partly a matter of capacity. NGDOs can make a strong contribution to building (grassroots) capacity. Up to now, however, the involvement of civil society (including NGDOs) has been limited (World Bank, 2000: 165).

Conditions for NGDO involvement in the process of democratisation

The two examples from India have shown that (theoretically) their strategies could lead to increasing democratisation, i.e. a situation in which the opportunities for people to get involved in the decision-making processes in their society are enhanced. There are certain conditions under which such a process can be stimulated by non-governmental organisations. The six most important conditions are discussed here.

The first was already mentioned: the setting up of a structure in which (representatives of) the government and people can meet. This 'structure' can take different forms, for instance the Coordination Committees set up by psu. It is important that in such a structure the NGDO should not be the main 'mouthpiece' of the target group. The target grouP itself (i.e. representatives of the target group) should be the most important partners of the government.

This brings us to a second important condition: organisation. NGDOs should promote the formation of groups and train leaders in representing these groups. Obviously, these groups should work in a democratic way and not become another possibility for already politically, economically, or otherwise powerful people to dominate and frustrate participation of others. It is exactly here that NGDOs should not surpass the existing Panchayati Raj Institutions and find appropriate ways of incorporating their 'own' groups into PRI. Moreover, in order to strengthen the democratic process in these grassroots organisations, the NGDO itself should provide opportunities for people to become involved in activities and strategies of, and decisions taken in the NGDO itself. In other words, a third condition is that the NGDOs are open to the participation of their target group in their own internal decision-making process (see CRD).

It will be clear that the above mentioned government - people structure is more likely to succeed in a society in which the government is willing to listen to and consider its citizens as political equals, and where the people have the resources to act as an equal partner of the government. This means that people should have the 'opportunities to 1) formulate their preferences; 2) signify their preferences to their fellow citizens and the government by individual and collective action; and 3) have their preferences weighed equally in the conduct of the government' (Sorensen, 1993: 12). In order to formulate their preferences, people need to be informed about their possibilities and the means to reach the preferences. Awareness-raising as a process, in which people achieve a better insight into their social, economic and political reality, and their possibilities for actively changing this reality, is therefore a fourth condition to which NGDOs should adhere.

Provision of information and education is a fifth condition, directly related to awareness-raising. Without access to information it will be impossible to become 'equal' partners to a government machinery. Information should be provided on the possibilities of government programmes and the ways of tapping those as well as on more basic issues such as literacy campaigns.

A sixth condition, transcending the individual NGDO level, is cooperation between NGDOS in order to strengthen the process of popular participation, and pressure on the government machinery. Although it appears that most NGDOs agree on this, it proves to be difficult to accomplish. Korten noted that '... one of the most serious barriers to expanding the development roles of NGDOs may be the difficulties they face in working with one another. Jealousies among them are often intense, and efforts at collaboration all too often break down into internecine warfare that paralyses efforts to work together towards the achievement of shared purposes' (cited in: Clark,1991: 92). In a survey among Indian NGDOs supported by the Dutch co-financing organisation ICCO, a large majority of NGDOs indicated that they had a regular (working) relation with other NGDOs. However, this relation was by most of them characterised as informal, i.e. without any fixed goals and strategies. Half of these ngdos stated that they experience problems in this relationship, ranging from differences in vision/ideology and in strategy/programmes to personality problems (Schulpen, 1994: 33-40).

Conclusion

Provided that the government is open to dialogue with its citizens and to active participation, NGDOs can play an important role in creating the conditions (together with the government and the people) for involvement of the people in decision-making processes within their society on a national level and certainly also on a regional and local level. NGDOs should not represent the target group, although they may do so in the beginning. In situations in which the government, is in principle, not open to dialogue and participation, NGDOs can still contribute to a more democratic society in the longer run through, for example, organisation and education of the people.

In order to successfully close the gap between the government (irrespective of whether the government is open to dialogue or not) and the people, and to contribute to a more democratic environment, NGDOs will have to fulfil certain conditions. The most important ones are awareness-raising, information provision and grassroots organisation, together with democratic operating of the NGDO and cooperation between NGDOs. In India, this would also include finding a way to deal with the PRI and, in the process, strengthening the panchayati structure in favour of the poor. Without the fulfilment of these conditions it will become very difficult (if not impossible) for an NGDO to contribute to the emergence of a sustainable system in which people can actively participate. The two organisations discussed briefly in this chapter (CRD in Andhra Pradesh and PSU in Uttar Pradesh) are both, in their own way, moving towards a type of NGDO that has the potential to transcend the local level. In both cases, however, the lack of strategic cooperation with other like-minded organisations reduces the impact of their programmes to a local level.

The structural changes sought by Korten's third generation of NGDOs are only possible if the conditions mentioned above are met. In short: 1) information, 2) organisation and 3) confrontation. Without the necessary information (be it concerning development programmes of the government aimed at poverty alleviation or concerning national or even international policies that could have an impact on the target group of the NGDO) and the organisation of the target group it will be impossible to move towards confrontation. This confrontation, despite the negative connotation, can be either destructive or constructive. Those NGDOs, which have concluded that 'government is bad' and should therefore be avoided, could be regarded as destructive. Constructive NGDOs are those which acknowledge that changing the structure of society (or even the structure of development programmes of that same government) is best done in dialogue.

NOTES

1. Advocacy is the term used to describe a cluster of activities aimed at influencing and altering opinions, decisions, structures and institutions which, in their different ways, impinge upon and influence development and development policies, and thus have an impact on the poor. The activities mentioned in this definition refer to, among other things, development and public education work, awareness-raising, lobbying, networking, dialogue and campaigning. See: Riddell, R. and the DWT (Discerning the Way Together) reference group. 1993: 41.
2. Not all organisations taken under the term donor NGDOs are by definition organisations which finance projects or programmes, or implement all

activities mentioned. To prevent confusion, all Northern NGDOs active in the field of development (either through fund raising, funding of project/ programmes, education and/or lobby) will be captured under the term donor NGDOs.

3. A division of NGDOs which is important in determining the influence on the policy of governments is a division on the basis of the working area or specialisation of the NGDOs. Although it seems that the majority of NGDOs implement a so-called integrated (or at least multi-component) programme, there are NGDOs which specialise in a specific area, like healthcare.
4. CAPART (Council for Advancement of People's Action and Rural Technology) was established in September 1986. CAPART is a so-called GONGDO (Government Organised NGDO) with as its objectives: 1) encourage, promote and assist voluntary action in the implementation of projects for the enhancement of rural prosperity; and 2) strengthen and promote voluntary efforts in rural development with a focus on injecting new technological inputs in this field. The primary task of CAPART is to provide financial assistance to NGDOs.
5. Holloway (1989: 7), for instance, stated that 'enlightened government departments do indeed have opportunities to help the poor and powerless, but experience has shown that low-level government functionaries, who actually interact with the poor in administering government programmes, find the alternative NGDO-type kind of development a threat to their status and livelihood and do not encourage them. There often seems to be a gulf between an official government statement and the actual behaviour of local functionaries who make some part of their living by controlling access to government services'.

8

PRIVATE DEVELOPMENT AID IN TRANSITION

— Fons van der Velden

The 1990s showed an enormous growth of non-governmental development organisations (NGDOs), both in the North and the South. The role of NGDOs, especially in their ability to reach the poor and promote their participation in the implementation of development programmes, was increasingly recognised by Western governments and multilateral institutions such as the World Bank, UNDP and UNICEF (see also Chapter 1). The 1990s, however, also showed a crisis of the dominant paradigm of development, resistance of the South against Western interference and a midlife crisis of Northern NGDOs. The question is how NGDOs, from North and South, should respond to these developments and safeguard their comparative advantages.

New Policy Agenda

The growth of the NGDO sector took place in a period in which development paradigms and policies changed significantly. The neo-liberal development model, which built on Rostow-style modernisation theories (Rostow, 1960), has become the dominant paradigm in the last decade. Its basic assumptions are: competition leads to economic progress and development; collective rationality follows from individual rationality; people act rationally; maximisation of profit in a perfect market is a universal value and leads to prosperity for everyone. Democracy according to the liberal democratic tradition follows from the tenet 'more market and less state'.

In the literature this is referred to as the New Policy Agenda. This agenda, of course, is not monolithic, as details differ from organisation to organisation. However, in almost all cases the policy of the organisations involved are, consciously or unconsciously, based on the twin concepts of neo-liberal economic and democratic theories (Hulme & Edwards, 1997a: 4-7).[1]

This approach has major consequences for current development cooperation. Schrijvers remarks:

> Development aid or development co-operation ... is not the soft sector with which professionals and scientists in this field are often associated. From the outset 'development' has been interwoven with major economic and political interests ... The predominant paradigm of 'development' still is, as in the colonial past, based on the belief in the supremacy of 'Western' man, 'Western' knowledge and technology, and of 'Western' civilisation as a whole (Schrijvers, 1997: 39-40).

The *New Policy Agenda* not only serves as the starting point for international development organisations such as the World Bank and IMF, but for Dutch policies as well. Virtually none of the political parties in the Netherlands have questioned the approach in their election manifesto. Nor does it hardly ever come into question in Dutch government policy. In concrete terms, the 1997 budget of the Ministry of Foreign Affairs, for instance, states that 'globalisation will expand, driven by technological innovation and the liberalisation of markets. The prospects for continued economic growth are favourable.' In the budget – which also provides for an increased role for the corporate sector – it is literally stated: 'If developing countries intend to be more fully integrated into the world economy, they should benefit more from the increasing availability of private capital. In addition to their own efforts, development aid could work as a catalyst and facilitate this process' (Ministerie van Buitenlandse Zaken, 1997: 2-3).[2] In terms of neo-liberal democracy, the plea made by the present Dutch Minister of Development Cooperation for good governance in sub-Saharan Africa may also lead to a pronounced European-based approach, to ethnocentrism.

Private development organisations, whether or not pressed by the financier, often adopt the prevalent predominant development model in their own policy. A number of mutually dependent factors are responsible for this incorporation (see for instance: James, 1997). Firstly, the retreat of the state. In the last few years there has been growing conviction that the government should reduce its direct role in economy and focus more on its role as facilitator of private initiatives. From the perspective of cost effectiveness the provision of basic social services to those who cannot be reached through the market mechanism should be left to NGDOs. Undoubtedly, private development organisations in the North and the South have many years of experience in the provision of social services. However, an important qualitative difference is that these organisations are now in principle considered the preferred channel for social services. It can therefore be said that a deliberate choice has been made for a systematic policy of substitution. In a great many countries with structural adjustment programmes, for example Tanzania, Zimbabwe and Bangladesh, governments encourage non-profit private initiatives to fill the gaps (Lewis, 1993; see also Chapter 1).[3]

Secondly, NGDOs are considered the main vehicles for the advancement of democratisation and essential components of civil society. The latter is of crucial importance to the realisation of the New Policy Agenda (Hulme & Edwards, 1997a: 5-6). In many countries in the South and Eastern Europe NGDOs are seen as a potentially important link between the state and the citizenry, and as a stimulus to – and part of – a pluralistic civil society (see Smillie & Helmich, 1994: 36).

Thirdly, in many countries there is a growing dissatisfaction with the effectiveness of governmental top-down development programmes, and the comparative advantage of NGDOs as instruments to facilitate bottom-up development is increasingly being recognised (see Fowler, 1997).

NGDOs as subcontractors

In theory these developments offer many opportunities for the not-for-profit private initiative. However, if the enormous expansion and recognition lead to a situation in which the agenda of NGDOs in the North and the South is increasingly being influenced or determined by other actors, then it is a high price to pay. As stated by Smillie (1995) and other commentators, NGDOs in the North and the South have increasingly become contractors, or even subcontractors, of big multilateral or national donor agencies. The organisations' own policies, often combined with pressure from their main financial source, are the most significant force bearing down on organisations to join the mainstream. Many non-governmental development organisations depend (or have become dependent) on private financing. As a result, the accountability mechanisms change and their autonomy is increasingly compromised.

In the literature this is often referred to as upward accountability: being accountable to, and satisfying the financier sometimes takes precedence over downward accountability (being accountable to the board, members and beneficiaries of the organisation itself) (Hulme & Edwards, 1997b)[4]. Increasingly the adage 'he who pays the piper calls the tune' holds true. It goes without saying that this development greatly affects the policy, instruments and workings of NGDOs. Moreover, it will reduce the diversity of the NGDO sector.

Similar tendencies can be observed in the Dutch development cooperation community. In recent years, for instance, the government has tightened the rules for the cooperating private organisations (including the four co-financing organisations) under the so-called Programme Financing Agreement. The increase in funds has gone hand in hand with stricter auditing. Another example is the India Committee in the Netherlands, originally an independent solidarity committee. Partly through the financier it directed its policy towards enhancing conditionality between bilateral and multilateral donor agencies (see Chapter 6). Belgian researchers further report that the policy of the Belgian chapter of Médecins sans Frontières is partly influenced by main financiers in the non-profit sector (the European Union and Nestlé, one of the main enterprises in the food industry) (Vandepitte et al., 1994:47-83).

The question is whether these developments constitute a positive impact on the effectiveness, efficacy and sustainability of NGDO activities in the North and the South.

The crisis of the dominant paradigm of development

The private sector has embraced the New Policy Agenda and for three reasons this is a paradoxical situation. In the first place, the 'Western civilisation project' is in serious crisis; secondly, Western dominance is heavily resisted, possibly more than ever; and thirdly, many private organisations in the North are experiencing a midlife crisis.

The crisis of the dominant paradigm of development is related to a range of factors which have insufficiently been addressed or taken into consideration in the prevailing development approach. First and foremost, it should be recognised that the Third World no longer exists. In his policy document A World of Difference, the then Minister of Development Cooperation of the Netherlands stated that: 'The distribution of wealth among nation states of which the world is composed is much more differentiated now compared to a few decades ago.' Some countries, that were rated among the 'underprivileged South' in the past, have succeeded in improving their position considerably; a number of the poorest countries seem to have been left behind. Within countries, both in the South and the North, a high degree of differentiation has taken place, so much so that it is increasingly appropriate to speak of 'discord' (Pronk, 1994: 183-185).

Secondly, in spite of the theoretical notions implicit in modernisation theory and the neo-liberal tradition, developing countries did not succeed in bridging the gap with the West. Although considerable progress has been made in the field of human development, large groups of the world population are still excluded, as is shown in publications from the United Nations Development Programme (UNDP).[5] Even in the most optimistic estimates regarding economic and population growth, more people in the Third World will live below the poverty line in the year 2000 than ever before. Moreover, the present maldevelopment goes hand in hand with an increase in different forms of violence: institutionalised violence from the top and responses to this violence from below (Schrijvers, 1993; 1997).

Thirdly, in recent years many developing countries have mainly directed their efforts to stay afloat through short-term policies aimed at repaying their debts without much attention to mid-term or long-term policies (Schuurman, 1992b: 18-19).

Two other factors have contributed to the crisis: in many instances disastrous environmental consequences of the prevailing development model were not foreseen, and the function and role of nation states have declined faster – and to a larger degree – than was generally assumed. 'The world market is an overarching entity beyond the control of nationally-oriented development policies' (Schuurman, 1992b: 19). Besides, the course of events in a number of countries in the South has made it increasingly clear that the international community cannot be as easily shaped according to a set of values as was thought twenty or thirty years ago. Furthermore, nowadays it is generally accepted that the role of international development cooperation is only of minor importance.

Criticism of the dominant paradigm: monoculture of the mind

The second reason why the private non-profit organisations' acceptance of the dominant development model, the New Policy Agenda, is paradoxical in the fierce criticism that, perhaps more than ever, has been voiced:

> Europeans display an exceptional inability to accept others as their equal, especially Africans. Once the principle of equality of both (value) systems is accepted, a dialogue can start. Currently, there is no dialogue at all because Europe does not accept the idea of alliance that presupposes equality with other cultures (Achebe, 1981: 371-372).[6]

Criticism of the modernisation discourse is not new. Scholars, for instance Wertheim, argued that emancipation[7] instead of modernisation should be the central issue (Wertheim, 1971). In his last book he stated:

> My main objection to the concept of 'modernisation' was that it all too easily implied a one-way process initiated from above by a leadership that derived its qualifications from acceptance of Western concepts and Western techniques. No process initiated from above takes roots without the actual involvement of the people concerned (…). Emancipation … is a process that does not develop in a unilinear, unambiguous way. Rather, it is a dialectic process, which advances in successive waves (Wertheim, 1997: 70).

Huizer was also among the early critics: 'The failure of the Western development model was most evident in the effects of the prevailing development policy on the majority of the poor' (Huizer, 1978: 14). In later publications he continued his criticism:

> … that 'free market' is being propagated and idealised; in fact a form of 'idolatry'. Human values hardly play a role

> and the attached no-nonsense mentality could be seen as a form of barbarism, in any case a form of anti-spirituality. A crucial question is whether it is possible to find and experience real spirituality ... whilst one is directly or indirectly, passively of actively an accessory to this anti-spirituality that has dominated our society in recent years (Huizer, 1992: 33; see also Huizer, 1994).

In other recent publications there is mention of the 'Economics of the madhouse' (Harman, 1997). Harman not only pays attention to processes of impoverishment in the South, but in the Western world as well (mass unemployment, growing poverty, great pressure on the environment, social division, increased feelings of insecurity among large parts of the population, pressure of work and stress among those who have secured a place in the citadel). He speaks about a 'madhouse' because 'the poverty in the world today is different. For it exists alongside wealth on a scale easily sufficient to banish poverty for ever' (Harman, 1997: 9-10).

The Ecumenical Movement Tomorrow, published under the auspices of the World Council of Churches, debunks the myth of the world as a global village in which people are all familiar with each other and share in the prosperity (Reuver, Solms & Huizer, 1992). In contrast to the world as a global village, there is 'fragmented globalisation' with sharp differences between the privileged and those who are excluded from participation in the world economy (Hamelink, 1993).

The neo-liberal development model has come under increasing fire not only in academic circles but also in societal organisations. Traditionally, progressive organisations, individuals and representatives of the political centre speak about 'predatory capitalism' (see Schmidt, 1998; Pronk, 1998a, 1998b).

It is striking that a United Nations agency, UNDP, has also engaged in this debate on values. The 1998 UNDP report on over-consumption by part of the world population, critically examines the 'grotesque' contrasts in the world and consumerism (UNDP, 1998). Galbraith, in an article on this report and looking back at the publication of his book *The Affluent Society* forty years ago, stated that 'the depressing difference in welfare between the affluent and the less fortunate' is not an economic problem:

> ... this goes down to a much deeper level of the human being. When people are fortunate in their individual well-being, and when countries are as fortunate, there is a general tendency to ignore the poor. Or they come up with another rationalisation for the happiness of the fortunate. The poor themselves are held responsible (Galbraith, 1998; see also Galbraith, 1992, for more extensive argumentation).

Last but not least, many scholars, social organisations and individuals from the South heavily criticise the dominant approach to development in the West and the accompanying norms and values (see Elizalde, 1993; Evers et al., 1993; Tandon, 1993). Basically, this criticism is not new; in 1854 Chief Seattle of the native American Dwamish tribe wondered about the implications arising from the strong emphasis on private ownership, for 'How can one possess the air?' (Seattle, 1980). A similar more recent consideration comes from the Indian environmentalist Vandana Shiva who speaks about the 'impoverished world view of the wealthy West', as a result of a monoculture of the mind:

> The ideology of 'civilising', which both justified and enabled Western dominance, is based on scientific and technical reductionism (Shiva, 1997: 89-102; see also Shiva, 1993).

Various ideological convictions from different parts of the world in the present and the past have warned against a premature and unconditional adoption and implementation of elements of the New Policy Agenda.

Based on similar considerations the British historian Davidson concludes: 'It is really too ridiculous for words to think that the West could offer the political solutions for Africa's problems' (Davidson, 1992a).[8] Many others made similar comments not only with reference to Africa but other continents as well (see Sizoo, 1992; van Nieuwenhuijze, 1993; Posthumus, 1997).

Midlife crisis and confusion of roles

Finally, there is a third reason why embracing the New Policy Agenda is paradoxical. Many NGDOs in the North and the South find themselves in a midlife crisis[9] and, as a result, are easy prey to cooptation by the establishment.

Looking back at the twentieth century, development cooperation may prove to be only a temporary phenomenon, or, as Breman puts it, 'a bridging of two eras marked by late-colonial politics in the first half of the century on the one hand, and the realisation of an integrated world economy organised on capitalist lines in this *fin de siècle,* on the other hand' (Breman, 1997: 26). This might happen indeed if the cooptation of the non-governmental sector continues in the same way and at the same speed.

In the debate and the issue of operational choices concerning the future of development cooperation, it is often forgotten that the state, the corporate sector and non-governmental development organisations in the North and South are guided by different sets of values and objectives. After all, conviction, vision and values are at the heart of every organisation from which other characteristics of the organisation are derived. To understand the natural role of the different actors in the development community, it is therefore important to make these central values more concrete. As for the state, ideally its tasks are to protect and assure the lives of its citizens and regulate society; 'Money and a lot more' is central to the corporate sector[10]; and in the NGDO sector more altruistic objectives prevail such as the care of fellow beings. The last-mentioned sector 'makes up the private realm for the pursuit of recreational, spiritual, social, cultural, and other personal or collective interests' (Fowler, 1997: especially chapter 1).[11] Fowler elaborates the fundamental differences between the different actors:

> Voluntary sector organisations do not have the legislative capacity and coercive force of the state, nor the economic clout of commercial capital and enterprise. What they have, instead, is the dynamism and power of self-willed human action, which can encompass very large numbers of people and exert significant influence in society ... (Fowler, 1997: 24).

Based on these differences in points of departure, NGDOs in the North and South have a number of comparative advantages vis-à-vis the 'first' and 'second' sectors: through their background, values, and involvement NGDO staff are closer to the target groups of development projects and programmes. Consequently, NGDOs are in a better position to contribute to developments from 'below'. As a rule, NGDOs are less bureaucratic and cumbersome than the government, and therefore, can respond more flexibly to local situations. In contrast to the corporate sector, NGDOs are better positioned to deal with the priorities of poor or marginalised groups because they mostly operate through the provision of subsidies rather than under market mechanisms. Their institutional flexibility makes it possible to engage in long-term relationships that in most cases are a prerequisite for sustainable development. Generally, NGDOs work more cost-effectively than business. Furthermore, NGDOs can supply important services that are less attractive to others (for instance facilitating networks, functioning as information channels and catalysts, political lobbying and advocacy (Fowler, 1997: 27-28).

In spite of these comparative advantages, it should be recognised that the three sectors are complementary and should balance each other.

Globalisation from below

In the light of the above-described comparative advantages and keeping in mind the identity and goals of the NGDO sector in general and the involved organisation in particular, development cooperation by private non-profit organisations from the North and South is aimed more at regulating and controlling current economic and political processes rather than facilitating them. It is their public duty:

> to steer the process [of globalisation], to counterbalance profit maximisation and give a voice to those who are excluded or downtrodden (Pronk, 1998a).

In short, it is not so much to promote private ownership but rather to denounce unequal property and income relations, to counter the unbridled abuse of power by the economic and political elite, to raise the issue of environmental degradation, to make a stand for human rights, and so on.

There is more. The meeting of cultures may lead to enrichment in many respects (see Pronk, 1994: 195-207). Rigoberta Menchu, the Guatamalan winner of the Nobel Prize for peace, stated that:

> Recognition of diversity and the building of an intercultural world are the challenges of the future (cited in Coolen, 1998: 5)

She further stresses that religion and spirituality should return to the agenda of the development debate (Coolen, 1998; Huizer, 1987; Huizer, 1992).

Huizer argues: 'Every historical development trend brings elements that may start a correction of the trend and sometimes lead to a counter movement' (Huizer, 1978: 190). Wertheim calls these elements counterpoints (Wertheim, 1964). In the debate on development as well as on the level of implementation NGDOs can play an important role as counterpoints.

In fact, the choices are simple. At the level of norms, just as Chambers contends, it is about people first; at the conceptual level it is about the notion that development does not imply a linear process that runs the same course everywhere; and at the empirical level development experts should realise that conditions are complex, differ from place to place, that the pace of change can vary significantly, that the poor often possess an enormous amount of knowledge and are perfectly able to organise themselves (Chambers, 1994: 1-14). For the NGDO sector this presents quite a challenge.

The current phase of globalisation, with all its technological developments, offers many opportunities and possibilities for the private development sector as well as churches to respond to the spiritual crisis in the West and play their part in the globalisation from below (Huizer, 1996). Until now their response leaves much to be desired. As Breman argues: 'It is not remarkable that capital is less bound to restrictions, but the absence of a counterbalance is remarkable indeed' (Breman, 1994). Recently De Gaay Fortman and Klein Goldewijk alleged that Catholic and Protestant churches have responded inadequately to the present-day crises (deepening poverty, environmental degradation and social disintegration) and they challenge the churches to cultivate a more pro-active attitude (De Gaay Fortman & Klein Goldewijk, 1998). The same plea could be made to the NGDO sector. There the point would be to regain the freedom or relative autonomy even when there is substantial government financing. NGDOs should strive not for cooptation but for a relatively independent position; otherwise they will become the 'ladles in the global soup kitchen' (Fowler, 1994). With respect to policy, issues such as intercultural communication, religion and spirituality, deserve more attention.

This would require – on the operational level – the NGDOs' strategic support for social organisations which act as a mediator between citizens and the government, and for organisations and institutions that strive for more democratic control and a greater say in local and international business. Besides, continuation of support in basic social services remains necessary, especially in sub-Saharan Africa. Influencing the policy in the NGDO source country is important in this respect. It should be carried out from an ecumenical and intercultural perspective 'as the substance of human dignity and common good is present in a great number of cultures, religions and churches' (Klein Goldewijk & Scheffers, 1998: 26).

Furthermore, established organisations should choose their modes of operation in such a way that they provide the opportunities for real two-way traffic and equality in the relationships between the North and South (Sizoo, 1992; Van der Velden & Zweers, 1997). In the Netherlands in particular the Dutch Association for Culture and Development (NVCO) has taken relevant initiatives to put this new form of development cooperation into practice:

> Respect for diversity on the one hand and recognition of the importance to meet in shared responsibilities on the other hand provides the only sustainable basis for international cooperation (Sizoo, 1992: 34).

As the consequences of globalisation penetrate further into the lives of people in the North and South, there will be a growing need for a response based on the joint norms and values that are present in the private non-profit sector. This is also globalisation, not top down but bottom up, with human dignity in the centre.

NOTES

1. Theoretically, according to a contemporary textbook on development studies, at least four views on development can be distinguished (see McGrew, 1992). A second view, next to neo-liberalism, is structuralism in which structures – not individuals – are taken as the point of departure. Neo-Marxists (who refer to classes) and dependency theorists (who emphasise the role of nations) are the main representatives of this tradition. Although the tradition has lost much influence in Western countries, this does not apply to Third World countries where the struggle between different social-political groups goes on.

   The third view encourages state intervention and regulation within the prevailing development model. Interventions and regulations should

counterbalance economic ups and downs, protect starting industries and reduce adverse social and environmental consequences.
In the fourth view people themselves are the agents of change. Participation and empowerment are key concepts. In the literature this tradition is often referred to as the approach of non-governmental development organisations or populism. (Main representatives are amongst others Robert Chambers, David Korten, Gerrit Huizer and Joke Schrijvers).

2. Many development agencies face the consequences of this approach in the implementation of their activities. For instance, with regard to staff support a plea is made to connect to and support economic processes that take place in the context of current globalisation. There should be a shift from more traditional sectors (education and health care) to civil society and good governance. 'Infrastructure for democracy' and in the economic field 'democratic infrastructure' are the terms used in this context.
3. For ideological and pragmatic reasons this is not without problems: NGDOs as a state within a state (see Chapter 1).
4. Upward accountability is characterised by rules: 'were the proper procedures followed?'; downward accountability vis-à-vis beneficiaries is usually translated as participation.
5. More than one billion people still live in absolute poverty and the income of the richest five per cent is150 times that of the poorest five per cent.
6. Cited in: Van de Werk, 1981.
7. Defined as 'any form of collective struggle on the part of groups that feel themselves to be treated as inferior or subordinate, fighting against privileges of the dominant groups' (Wertheim, 1997:69-70).
8. For more than forty years Davidson has investigated the cultural history of Africa. In *The black man's burden: Africa and the curse of the nation state* (1992b) he reaches the conclusion that imported models such as the nation state do not do justice to historically determined local situations and are doomed to end in utter failure. The same arguments may be used for the current export of the New Policy Agenda. In this context reference can also be made to Adebayo Adedeji who argues that Fukuyama wrongly takes it for granted that there is a direct linear relation between neo-liberal democracy and the neo-liberal economic development model (Adedeji & Otite, 1997).
9. For further details of this proposition see Van der Velden 1994a; Bossuyt, 1993; Hulme & Edwards, 1997a; and Chapter 1.
10. In the 1995 jubilee edition *Money and a lot more* of the Netherlands Development Finance Company symbolises this trend (Dalmeyer, 1995).
11. In reality the distinction is of course less rigid and areas in which goals and activities overlap do exist.

BIBLIOGRAPHY

ABOS (1999) *De partnerrelatie van de NGO's: uitdagingen en vooruitzichten van de Belgische NGO's, medegefinancierd op de begroting ontwikkelingssamenwerking*, Brussel, Algemeen Bestuur van de Ontwikkelingssamenwerking.

Achebe, C. (1981) *Pijl van God, Amsterdam*, Amsterdam, Rainbow pocketboeken (first edition: 1964).

Achterhuis, H. (1973) *De uitgestelde revolutie; Over ontwikkeling en apartheid*, Baarn, Anthos.

Achterhuis, H. *et al.* (1993) *Het orkest van de Titanic; Werken aan andere Noord-Zuid verhoudingen*, Brussel/Leuven, VUBPRESS/Student Aid.

Adedeji, A. and O. Otite (eds.) (1997) *Nigeria: renewal from the roots; The struggle for democratic development*, London, Zed Books.

Arts, B. (1998) *The political influence of global NGOs - case studies on the climate and biodiversity conventions*, Utrecht, International Books.

Barrez, D. (1993) De Val der Engelen; waarom ontwikkelingsorganisaties falen, in: H. Achterhuis, *et al.*, *Het orkest van de Titanic; Werken aan andere Noord-Zuid verhoudingen*, Brussel/Leuven, VUBPRESS/Student Aid, pp. 37- 117.

Beerends, H. (1993) *De Derde Wereldbeweging; Geschiedenis en toekomst*, Utrecht, Jan van Arkel.

Beets, N., J. Neggers and F. Wils (1988) *Big and still beautiful, enquiry into the efficiency and effectiveness of three big NGOs (BINGOS) in South Asia*, The Hague, DGIS programme evaluation.

Bering, E. *et al.* (1989) *The Danish NGO evaluation – Non-governmental actions: a necessary and growing option*, Kopenhagen, Danida/CASA, November.

Biekart, K. (1999) *The politics of civil society building - European private aid agencies and democratic transitions in Central America*, Utrecht/Amsterdam, International Books/Transnational Institute.

Bol, D. (1978) Ontwikkelingssamenwerking: wie helpt wie?, in: G. Huizer (ed.), *Nederland en de Derde Wereld; basisvragen over ontwikkelingssamen-werking*, Alphen aan de Rijn/Brussel, Samsom. pp. 63-94.

Bossuyt, J. (1993) De midlife crisis van de NGO-sector, in: H. Achterhuis, et al., *Het orkest van de Titanic; Werken aan andere Noord-Zuid verhoudingen*, Brussel/Leuven, VUBPRESS/Student Aid, pp. 201-216.

Breman, L. (1994) De verzorgingsstaat is van de wereld, in: *De Volkskrant*, 29 October.

Breman, J. (1997) Armoedebestrijding in het kader van de globalisering, in: K. Lieten & F. van der Velden (eds.), *Grenzen aan de hulp; beleid en effecten van ontwikkelingssamenwerking*, Amsterdam, Spinhuis, pp. 17-37.

Broadhead, T. (1987) NGDOs: in one year, out the other?, in: *World Development*, Vol. 15 (supplement), September: pp. 1-6.

Buck, M., *et al.* (1982) *ICCO in India, Programme evaluation*, The Hague (DGIS).

Burnell, P. (1991) *Charity, politics and the Third World*, Herfordshire, Harvester Wheatsheaf.

Caroll, T.F. (1992) *Intermediary NGOs: the supporting link in grassroots development*, West Hartford, Kumarian Press.

Cassen, R. (1994) *Does aid work?: report to an intergovernmental task force*, Oxford, Clarendon Press (second edition).

Chambers, R. (1985) Putting 'last' thinking first: a professional revolution, in: A. Gauhar (ed.), *Third World Affairs 1985*, London, Third World Foundation for Social and Economic Studies, pp. 78-94.

Chambers, R. (1992) *Rural Appraisal: Rapid, Relaxed and Participatory*, Brighton, IDS (Discussion Paper 311).

Chambers, R. (1993) *Challenging the Professionals, Frontiers for rural development*, London, Intermediate Technology Publications.

Chambers, R. (1995) Paradigm shifts and the practice of participatory research and development, in: N. Nelson and S. Wright (eds.) *Power and Participatory Development – theory and practice*, London, Intermediate Technology Publications.

Chambers, R. *et al.* (1983) *Rural Development; Putting the last first*, Essex,

Longman.

Chambers, R., N.C. Saxena and Shah, T (1989) *To the hands of the poor: Water and Trees*, New Delhi, Oxford & IBH.

Chandy, Fr. K.T. S.J. *et al.* (1991) *Matching poverty alleviation and sustainable land use*, Wageningen/New Delhi (draft).

Chomsky, N. (1993) *The Year 501: The Conquest Continues*, London, Verso.

Clark, J. (1991) *Democratizing Development - the role of voluntary organisations*, London, Earthscan Publications.

Clayton A. (ed.) (1994) *Governance, Democracy & Conditionality: What Role for NGOS?*, Oxford, INTRAC.

Coolen, M. (1998) *Een rozentuin vol wijsheid; Indiase spiritualiteit als uitdaging*, Heeswijk, Dabar-Luyten.

Dalmeyer, M.C.M. (ed.) (1995) *Geld en nog veel meer; 25 jaar beleid en praktijk van investeren in ontwikkeling*, Den Haag, SDU.

Davidson, B. (1992a) Basil Davidson over Afrika; Het kolonialisme was politiek en moreel een absolute ramp, in: *Onze Wereld*, November, pp. 20-23. (Interview by P. van den Akker.)

Davidson, B. (1992b) The black man's burden: Africa and the curse of the nation-state, New York, Times Books.

De Gaay Fortman, B. and B. Klein Goldewijk (1998) *God and the Goods; Global economy in a civilization perspective*, Geneva, WCC Publications.

De Jong, E. (1998) *Naar gelijkwaardige partners?!; Aanzetten tot een christelijk geïnspireerde visie op de positie van arme landen*, Assen, Van Gorcum.

De Jonge, F. (1998) De moraal is van ons allemaal, in: *De Volkskrant*, 14 February.

Drabek, A. (1987) Development alternatives: the challenge for NGDOs - an overview of the issues, in: World Development, Vol. 15 (supplement), September: pp. ix-xv.

Dramé, T. (1995) The crisis of the state, in: S. Ellis (ed.) *Africa Now; People, Policies and Institutions*, The Hague/London, Ministry of Foreign Affairs/ James Currey, pp. 201-211.

Dutch Association for Culture and Development (1996) *Mutuality in South*

– North Cooperation; If you don't understand us, listen to the cries of the people in your own society, Amersfoort, NVCO.

Edwards, M. and Hulme, D. (eds.) (1992) *Making a difference: NGOs and development in a changing world*, London, Earthscan Publications.

Edwards, M. and Hulme, D. (eds.) (1995) *Non-governmental organisations - performance and accountability: beyond the magic bullet*, London, Earthscan Publications.

Elizalde, A. (1993) De NGO's en de internationale samenwerking; Een fenomenologische benadering van het thema, in: H. Achterhuis, *et al.*, *Het orkest van de Titanic; Werken aan andere Noord-Zuid verhoudingen*, Brussel/Leuven, VUBPRESS/Student Aid, pp. 161-180.

Evers, F., K. de Pater, B. Posthumus and L. Schout (1993) *Verslag "Open voor Afrika" World Trade Centre Rotterdam 1 april 1993*, Den Haag/Amsterdam, HIVOS/Inzet.

Farrington, J. and A. Bebbington, *et al.* (1993) *Reluctant partners? Non-Governmental organisations, the state and sustainable agricultural development*, London/New York, Routledge.

Fowler, A. (1988) *Non-governmental organisations in Africa: Achieving comparative advantage in relief and micro-development*, Sussex, Institute of Development Studies (Discussion Paper 249).

Fowler, A. (1992) Prioritising institutional development: A new role for NGO centres for study and development, in: *The Gate Keepers Series*, No. 35, London, IIED.

Fowler, A. (1994) Capacity Building and NGOs; A case of the strengthening ladles for the global soup kitchen, in: *Institutional Development (New Delhi)*, Vol.1, No.1.

Fowler, A.F. (1996) *Authentic partnership in the new policy agenda for international aid: dead end or light ahead?*, Paper presented at the TNI workshop 'Re-inventing solidarity: Private foreign aid reconsidered', Amsterdam, June.

Fowler, A. (1997) *Striking a balance - a guide to enhancing the effectiveness of non-governmental organisations in international development*, London, Earthscan Publications.

Fowler, A. and Biekart, K. (1996), Do private agencies really make a difference?, in: Sogge, D. (ed.), *Compassion & calculation - the business of private foreign aid*, London/Amsterdam, Pluto Press/ Transnational Institute.

Galbraith, J. (1992) *The culture of contentment*, London, Sinclair-Stevens, 1992.

Galbraith, J. (1998) Rijke mensen genieten van hun welvaart zonder last van hun geweten, in: *Trouw*, 10 September.

GOM (1995) *Met het oog op kwaliteit – eindrapportage over de maatregelen van Cebemo, Hivos, Icco en Novib naar aanleiding van de Impactstudie*, Oegstgeest, GOM, March.

Hamelink, C.J. (1993) Our common information future: Does it matter?, in: M. Reuver *et al.*, *The ecumenical movement tomorrow; Suggestions for approaches and alternatives,* Kampen/Geneva, Kok Publishing House/WCC Publications, pp. 57-67.

Hancock, G. (1991) *Lords of poverty*, London, Mandarin.

Handelingen van de Tweede Kamer 1992-1993, 22 549, no. 6, pp. 2 and 12.

Hardeman, J. *et al.* (1992) *Armoede voorbij*, Zeist, (internal working document ICCO).

Haijtink, A. and P. Hoebink (1998) Financiering van ontwikkeling: ontwikkelingshulp, particuliere stromen en schulden, in: E. de Jong, *Naar gelijkwaardige partners?!; Aanzetten tot een christelijk geïnspireerde visie op de positie van arme landen,* Assen, Van Gorcum, pp. 86-105.

Harman, C. (1997) *Economics of the madhouse; Capitalism and the market today*, London, Bookmarks (first edition: 1995).

Hettne, B. (1990), *Development theory and the three worlds*, New York, Longman Development Studies.

Hewitt A.P. (1994) *Crisis or Transition in Foreign Aid*, London/ Washington/Ottawa, ODI.

Hoebink, P. (1995) *De Effectiviteit van de Hulp*, Den Haag, Ministerie van Buitenlandse Zaken.

Hoebink, P. (1997) Ontwikkelingshulp van staat tot staat, in: K. Lieten & F. van der Velden (eds.), *Grenzen aan de hulp; beleid en effecten van ontwikkelingssamenwerking*, Amsterdam, Spinhuis.

Hoebink, P. and L. Schulpen (1998) *Netherlands aid policies for poverty reduction*, London, Overseas Development Institute, Working

Paper 115.

Hoebink, P. & L. Schulpen (1999) *Evaluation and conditionality in the NGDO-network: no strings for shoestrings? - lessons and non-lessons from 'Assesssing Aid' for NGDOs,* Paper presented at the 'Assessing Aid' workshop, University of Groningen, December.

Holloway, R. (ed.) (1989) *Doing development: governments, NGDOs and the rural poor in Asia*, London, Earthscan Publications.

Huizer, G. (ed.) (1978) *Nederland en de Derde Wereld; basisvragen over ontwikkelingssamenwerking*, Alphen aan de Rijn/Brussel, Samsom.

Huizer, G. (1987) Christendom moet zich openstellen voor boodschap inheemse kultuur, in: *Solidaridad Blad*, 187/4. (Interview by G. van Rheenen and R. van de Bijl).

Huizer, G. (1992) *Leren van de Derde Wereld; Crisis als uitdaging*, Kampen, Kok Agora.

Huizer, G. (1994) Indigenous knowledge and popular spirituality: a challenge to developmentalists, in: F. Schuurman (ed.), *Current issues in development studies*, Saarbrücken, Verlag für Entwicklungspolitik Breitenbach, pp. 56-90.

Huizer, G. (1996) Social movements in the underdevelopment of development dialectic. A view from below, in: S.C. Chew and R.A. Denemark, *The underdevelopment of development. Essays in honor of Andre Gunder Frank*, Thousand Oaks/London/NewDelhi, Sage, pp. 281-313.

Hulme, D. and Edwards, M. (eds.) (1997a), *NGOs, states and donors; too close for comfort?*, London, Macmillan.

Hulme, D. and M. Edwards (1997b) NGOs, states and donors: an overview, in: Hulme, D. and M. Edwards (eds.) (1997) *NGOs, states and donors; too close for comfort*, London, MacMillan/Save the Children.

Huy, A. (1995) Pramada Menon contra opdringerige donoren; 'Waarom is een dialoog toch zo moeilijk…?', in: *Inzet*, December, pp. 10-11.

ICCO (1977) *10 Year report*, Utrecht, ICCO, April.

ICCO (1984) *Terugblik India 1980-1983 (een verslag dat meer is dan een terugblik)*, Utrecht, ICCO, January (internal document).

ICCO (1986) *Justice and Mercy - starting points for policy*, Zeist, ICCO.

ICCO (1987a) *Some notes on ICCO's policy and involvement in India (introductory paper)*, Zeist, ICCO, August (internal document).

ICCO (1987b) *Annual Report 1986*, Zeist, ICCO.

ICCO (1988) *Annual Report 1987*, Zeist, ICCO.

ICCO (1989) *ICCO op weg naar het jaar 2000*, Zeist, ICCO, May (internal document).

ICCO (1990) *India - beleidsnotitie*, Zeist, ICCO (India desk), August (internal document).

ICCO (1993a) *Tekenen van hoop - opdracht en beleid van ICCO,* Zeist, ICCO , December.

ICCO (1993b) *ICCO Policy Profile India 1993-1995*, Zeist, ICCO, April (internal document).

ICCO (1998) *Policy Profile India 1998-2002*, Zeist, South Asia Desk/ ICCO.

Inspectie Ontwikkelingssamenwerking te Velde (1994*) Evaluatie van de Nederlandse hulp aan India, Mali en Tanzania*, Den Haag, Ministerie van Buitenlandse Zaken.

India Nieuwsbrief (1986a) No. 43, July-August.

India Nieuwsbrief (1986b) No. 44, September-October.

James, R. (1997) *Partnership through capacity-building: advocacy with integrity*, Oxford, INTRAC.

Jepma, C.J. (1995*) On the Effectiveness of Development Aid; A survey of the main recent findings in the academic literature on the impact and effectiveness of development aid and related transfers*, Den Haag, Ministerie van Buitenlandse Zaken.

Klein Goldewijk B., B. and V. Scheffers (1998) Het primaat van de sociale ethiek, in: E. de Jong, *Naar gelijkwaardige partners?!; Aanzetten tot een christelijk geïnspireerde visie op de positie van arme landen*, Assen, Van Gorcum, pp. 13-29.

Kolko, G. & J. (1972) *The Limits of Power, the World and United States Foreign Policy 1945 - 1954*, New York, Harper and Row.

Korten, D. (1987) Third generation NGDO strategies: a key to people-centred development, in: *World Development*, Vol. 15 (supplement), September: pp. 145-159.

Korten, D. (1990) *Getting to the 21st century: voluntary action and the global agenda*, West Hartford, Kumarian Press.

Kruijt, D, K. Koonings and M. Vellinga (1983) De Nederlandse Ontwikkelingsgemeenschap, in: D. Kruijt and M. Vellinga (eds.), *Ontwikkelingshulp getest: resultaten onder de loep*, Muiderberg, Coutinho, pp. 11-40.

Kruijt, D. and M. Vellinga (eds.) (1983), *Ontwikkelingshulp getest: resultaten onder de loep*, Muiderberg, Coutinho.

Landelijke India Werkgroep (1981) *'Blauwe revolutie' in India; miljoenen vissers bedreigd door opmars trawlers*, Utrecht, Landelijke India Werkgroep.

Landelijke India Werkgroep (1982) *De Nederlandse kunstmest hulp/ handel aan India*, Utrecht, Landelijke India Werkgroep.

Landelijke India Werkgroep (1985) *India als melkkoe van de EG*, Utrecht, Landelijke India Werkgroep.

Landelijke India Werkgroep (1990) *Werk tegen armoede; een ander ontwikkelingsbeleid voor 100 miljoen Indiase landlozen*, Utrecht, Landelijke India Werkgroep.

Lap, B. (1994) *North - South relationships beyond development cooperation*, Paper for the joint assembly of Caritas Asia/Oceania and Justice and Peace Committees of Asia, Bangkok.

Lap, B. (1997) Partnership, niets dan een illusie?, in: K. Lieten and F. van der Velden (eds.) *Grenzen aan de hulp; beleid en effecten van ontwikkelingssamenwerking*, Amsterdam, Spinhuis.

Lewis, D.J. (1993) Overview, in: J. Farrington and D. J. Lewis, *Non-Governmental organisations and the state in Asia*, London/New York, Routledge, pp. 47-58.

Lieten, G.K. (1992) *Continuity and change in rural West Bengal*, New Delhi, Sage.

Lieten, K. and F. van der Velden (eds.) (1997)), *Grenzen aan de hulp; beleid en effecten van ontwikkelingssamenwerking*, Amsterdam, Spinhuis.

Lloyd, T. (1993) *The Charity Business: The new philanthropists*, London, John Murray.

Mathew, G. (1994) *Panchayati Raj - from legislation to movement*, New Delhi, Concept Publishing Company.

McGrew, A. (1992) The Third World in the New Global Order, in: T.

Allen and A. Thomas (eds.), *Poverty and development in the 1990s*, Oxford, Oxford University Press, pp.255-273.

Miltenburg, J. (1978) De Derde-Wereldbeweging in Nederland: van morele verontwaardiging tot anti-imperialisme, in: Huizer, G. (ed.), *Nederland en de Derde Wereld; basisvragen over ontwikkelingssamenwerking*, Alphen aan den Rijn/Brussel, Samsom.

Ministerie van Buitenlandse Zaken (1991) *A world of difference - a new framework for development cooperation in the 1990s*, Den Haag, Ministerie van Buitenlandse Zaken, March.

Ministerie van Buitenlandse Zaken (1992) *India; Beleidsplan voor de periode 1992-1995*, Den Haag, Ministerie van Buitenlandse Zaken.

Ministerie van Buitenlandse Zaken (1996) *Hulp in uitvoering – ontwikkelingssamenwerking en de herijking van het buitenlands beleid,* Den Haag, Ministerie van Buitenlandse Zaken.

Ministerie van Buitenlandse Zaken (1997) *Begroting Buitenlandse Zaken/ Ontwikkelingssamenwerking*, Den Haag, Ministerie van Buitenlandse Zaken.

Ministerie van Buitenlandse Zaken (1998) *Begroting Buitenlandse Zaken/ Ontwikkelingssamenwerking*, Den Haag, Ministerie van Buitenlandse Zaken.

Ministerie van Buitenlandse Zaken (1999a) *De kwaliteit van de Europese hulp*, Den Haag, Ministerie van Buitenlandse Zaken, May.

Ministerie van Buitenlandse Zaken (1999b) *Gesprek Herfkens met MFO's (press communication)*, Den Haag, Voorlichtingsdienst Ontwikkelingssamen-werking, 25 February.

Nath, N.C.B. (1989) *NGOs and Indian Development Effort*, New Delhi, FAIR.

Nayyar, D. (1975) *Economic Relations between socialist countries and the Third World*, London, Macmillan.

Negash, G. and E. Djene (1993) *Fourth reversal project; An investigation into the representation of the South, and especially Africa, by seven Dutch agencies*, Utrecht, Andersom.

Nissen, B. (1975) Building the World Bank, in: S. Weissman *et al.* (1975) *The Trojan Horse; A Radical Look at Foreign Aid*, Palo Alto, Ramparts Press, pp. 35-61.

Oman, C.P. and Wignaraja, G. (1991) *Post war evolution of development thinking*, London, Macmillan.

Oonk, G. (1992) Ontwikkelingshulp: geen blanco cheque; kritiek op campagne 'Werk tegen Armoede' misplaatst, in: *India Nu*, May-June.

Oakley, P. (1994) *People's participation in development; Reviewing the balance sheet*, Paper presented at the workshop NGOs and Participation: Bridging the gap between rhetoric and reality, INTRAC, Oxford, June.

Oakley, P. (1999) *The Danish NGO Impact Study – a review of Danish NGO activities in developing countries – overview report*, Oxford, INTRAC, September.

Patni, R. (1990) *Wage structures and issues in HRD in the voluntary sector: Some preliminary findings*, New Delhi, Foundation to Aid Industrial Recovery.

Payer, C. (1975) The IMF and the Third World, in: S. Weissman et al. (1975) *The Trojan Horse; A Radical Look at Foreign Aid*, Palo Alto, Ramparts Press, pp. 61-73.

Petras, J. (1993) Cultural Imperialism in the Late 20th Century, in: *Journal of Contemporary Asia*, Vol. 23 (2), pp. 139-148.

Petras, J. (1996) Social Scientists, NGOs and Intellectuals, in: *Lanka Guardian*, No. 11, October.

Postumus, B. (ed.) (1997) *Making moral choices in development cooperation; Conference report on Ethics and Development, March 20-22*, Kontakt der Kontinenten, Soesterberg, Soesterberg, NVCO.

Pronk, J.P. (1990) *Een wereld van verschil; Nieuwe kaders voor ontwikkelingssamenwerking in de jaren negentig* (Tweede Kamer der Staten-Generaal, vergaderjaar 1990-1991, 21 813, no. 1-2).

Pronk, J.P. (1994) *De kritische grens; Beschouwingen over tweespalt en orde*, Amsterdam, Prometheus.

Pronk, J.P. (1998a) Tegen de transnationale hebzucht, in: *De Groene Amsterdammer*, 7 January.

Pronk, J.P. (1998b) De globalisering is op hol geslagen en verdient bijsturing, in: *NRC Handelsblad*, 25 April.

Put, M. (1998) *Innocent farmers?: a comparative evaluation into a government and NGO project located in semi-arid Andhra Pradesh (India), meant to induce farmers to adopt innovations for dryland agriculture*, Amsterdam, Thela Publishers.

Quarles van Ufford, Ph., D. Kruijt, and T. Downing, (eds.) (1988) *The Hidden Crisis in Development: Development Bureaucracies*, Tokyo/Amsterdam, United Nations University Press/Free University Press.

Quarles van Ufford, Ph. and F. Wils (1991) *Kwaliteitszorg in de jaren 1990*, Den Haag, Novib.

Quarles van Ufford, Ph. (1995) Ontwikkelingssamenwerking als probleem van organisatie, in: R.D. van den Bergh and Ph. Quarles van Ufford (red.) *De toekomst van de Nederlandse ontwikkelingssamenwerking; bijdragen aan een inhoudelijk debat*, Utrecht/Woubrugge, Mets/Agora, pp. 131-151.

Reuver, F., F. Solms & G. Huizer (eds.) (1992) *The ecumenical movement tomorrow; Suggestions for approaches and alternatives*, Kampen/Geneva, Kok/WCC Publications.

Rinnooy Kan, A.H.G. (1993) De rol van het bedrijfsleven in de vermaatschappelijking van de hulp, in: R.F.M. Lubbers et al., *Het Nederlandse Ontwikkelingsbeleid in de Tweede Helft van de Jaren Negentig*, Amsterdam, SID/NCO/KIT, pp. 31-44.

Riddell, R.C. (1987) *Foreign Aid Reconsidered, Baltimore*, Johns Hopkins University Press.

Riddell, R. & M. Robinson (1992) *The impact of NGO poverty alleviation projects: results of the case study and evaluations*, London, Overseas Development Institute (Working Paper 68).

Riddell, R. and the DWT (Discerning the Way Together) reference group (1993) *Discerning the way together: report on the work of Brot für die Welt, Christian Aid, EZE and ICCO*, July, London, mimeo.

Riddell R. *et al.* (1994) *Strengthening the Partnership; Evaluation of the Finnish NGO Support Programme*, Helsinki, Finnida.

Riddell, R. and Robinson, M. (1995) *Non-Governmental Organisations and rural poverty alleviation*, London/Oxford, Overseas Development Institute/Clarendon Press.

Ridker, R.G. (1994) *The World Bank's Role in Human Resource Development in Sub-Saharan Africa: Education, Training and Technical Assistance*, Washington D.C., World Bank.

Robinson, M.A. (1991) *Evaluating the impact of NGOs in rural poverty alleviation - India country study*, London, Overseas Development Institute (ODI working paper 49), October.

Rostow, W. (1960) *The stages of economic growth; A non-communist manifesto*, London, Cambridge University Press.

Sachs, W. (1992) Introduction, in: W. Sachs (ed.), *The Development Dictionary; A guide to Knowledge as Power*, Johannesburg/ London, Witwatersrand University Press/Zed Books Ltd, pp. 1-5.

Schiel, T. (1987) 'Entbürokratisierung' der Entwicklungshilfe? - Ueber die Grensen von Nichtregierungsorganisationen und die Ullusion staatsferner Entwicklungshilfen, in: *Peripherie*, No. 25/26: pp. 79-92.

Schmidt, H. (1998) Wie temt het roofdierkapitalisme, in: *De Volkskrant*, 12 September.

Schrijvers, J., L. Pugh and N. Majaraj (1993) *The violence of 'development': a choice for intellectuals*, Utrecht/New Delhi, International Books/Kali for Women.

Schrijvers, J. (1997) Ontwikkelingsparadigma's; Een kritisch perspectief, in: K. Lieten & F. van der Velden (eds.) (1997) *), Grenzen aan de hulp; beleid en effecten van ontwikkelingssamenwerking,* Amsterdam, Spinhuis, pp. 39-60.

Schulpen, L. (1991) NGDO's en de 'bende van vier' in een 'Wereld van verschil, in: *Derde Wereld*, jrg. 10, No. 3, December: pp. 4-6.

Schulpen, L. (1994) *Beyond the target-group ... - Indian NGDOs on ICCO, the government and themselves*, Nijmegen, September (unpublished report of a survey among ICCO-counterparts in India).

Schulpen, L. (1997) *The same difference - a comparison of Dutch aid channels to India*, Saarbrücken, Breitenbach.

Schulpen, L. (1998) Participatie in ontwikkelingsprojecten, in: E. de Jong (ed*.), Naar gelijkwaardige partners?! – aanzetten tot een christelijk geïnspireerde visie op de positie van arme landen*, Assen, Van Gorcum.

Schulpen, L and F. van der Velden (1992) Medefinanciering in de praktijk: het ICCO programma in India, in: *Internationale Spectator*, September, pp. 481 - 489.

Schulte Nordholt, N.G. (1992) *Achtergronden van de breuk tussen*

Indonesië en Nederland; Hoe nu verder?, SID-KIT bijeenkomst, Amsterdam, 14 April.

Schulte Nordholt, N.G. (1995) Aid and Conditionality; The Case of Dutch-Indonesian Relationships, in: Stokke, O. (ed.), *Aid and Political Conditionality*, London, Frank Cass, pp. 129-161.

Schuurman, F. (1992a) Niet-Gouvernementele Organisaties in Chili, in: *NGDO country study, Impactstudy co-financing Programme, Latin America: Brasil, Chile,* Utrecht, Libertas: pp. 40-63.

Schuurman, F. (1992b) Post-impasse ontwikkelingstheorieën, in: *Derde Wereld*, Vol. 12, No. 1, pp. 9-51.

Seattle (1980) *Hoe kun je de lucht bezitten; een Indiaanse visie op het beheer van de aarde*, Utrecht, Aktie Strohalm/Ekologische Uitgeverij.

Shah, G. (1991) *Non-Governmental Organisations in India; NGO Landenstudie India/Impactstudie Medefinancieringsprogramma*, Oegstgeest, GOM.

Shiva, V. (1988) *Staying alive: Women, Ecology and Survival in India*, New Delhi, Kali for Women.

Shiva, V. (1993) *Monocultures of the mind; Biodiversity, Biotechnology and the Third World*, Penang, Third World Network.

Shiva, V. *et. al.* (1997) *De armoedige levensvisie van het rijke Westen; Milieu en Derde-Wereldproblemen: het resultaat van een geestelijke monocultuur*, Baarn, Ten Have.

Sizoo, E. (ed.) (1992) *Ontwikkelingssamenwerking voorbij; Naar een cultuurbewuste benadering*, Soesterberg, Dutch Association for Culture and Development.

Sizoo, E. (ed.) (1993) *Beyond development cooperation; towards a culture-conscious approach*, Soesterberg, Dutch Association for Culture and Development.

Smillie, I and Helmich, H. (eds.) (1994) *Non-Governmental Organisations and Governments: stakeholders for development*, Paris, OECD.

Smillie, I. (1995) *The Alms Bazaar; Altruism under fire – Non-profit organisations and international development*, London, Intermediate Technology Publications.

Smith, B. (1990) *More than altruism: the politics of private foreign aid*, Princeton University Press.

Sogge, D. (ed.) (1996) *Compassion & calculation - the business of private foreign aid*, London/Amsterdam, Pluto Press/Transnational Institute.

Sorensen, G. (1993) *Democracy and democratisation - processes and prospects in a changing world*, Oxford, Westview Press.

South Commission (1990) *The challenge to the South; The report of the South Commission*, Geneva, South Commission.

Steering Group Impact Co-financing Programme (1991) *Significance of the Co-financing Programme: An Exploration*, Oegstgeest, GOM.

Steering Committee Impact Study (1991) *Impact assessment of the Co-financing Programme: an exploration*, Oegstgeest, September.

Stephen, F. (1989) *NGOs - Hope of the last decade of this century!*, Bangalore, SEARCH.

Stephen, F. (1994) *Cooperation and Complementarity Among European Agencies*, Paper presented at the ICCO conference Discerning the Way Together, Bangalore.

Stiefel, M. and M. Wolfe (1994) *A voice for the excluded - popular participation in development: utopia or necessity?*, London, Zed Books/UNRISD.

Tandon, Y. (1993) Buitenlandse NGO's; Gebruiken en misbruiken vanuit een Afrikaans perspectief, in: H. Achterhuis et al., *Het orkest van de Titanic; Werken aan andere Noord-Zuid verhoudingen*, Brussel/ Leuven, VUBPRESS/Student Aid, pp. 117-132.

Taylor, M. (1995) *Not Angles but Agencies; The Ecumenical Response to Poverty - A Primer*, London/Geneva, SCM Press/WCC Publications.

Teerink, R., P. Viegas and L. Schenk-Sandbergen (1991) *Jamkhed: flowers in the dust*, Amsterdam, Centre for Asian Studies.

Thérien, J. P. (1991) Non-Governmental Organisations and international development assistance, in: *Canadian Journal of Development Studies*, vol. XII, No. 2: pp. 263-280.

Tims, W. (1995) Samenwerken met ontwikkelingslanden; Omstreden noodzaak, in: *Internationale Spectator*, november, pp. 579-584.

Tijdschrift Anti-Imperialisme Scholing (1973) *Nederlandse ontwikkelingshulp in dienst van kapitaalsbelangen.*

Update Collective (1992) *A campaign against poverty*, Update from Delhi,

29 November.

United Nations (Department for Economic and Social Information and Policy Analysis) (1995) *World Economic and Social Survey 1995; Current Trends and Policies in the World Economy*, New York, United Nations.

UNDP (1990), *Human Development Report 1990*, New York/Oxford, Oxford University Press.

UNDP (1991) *Human Development Report 1991*, New York/Oxford, Oxford University Press.

UNDP (1992) *Human Development Report 1992*, New York/Oxford, Oxford University Press.

UNDP (1993) *Human Development Report 1993*, New York/Oxford, Oxford University Press.

UNDP (1994) *Human Development Report 1994*, New York/Oxford, Oxford University Press.

UNDP (1998) *Human Development Report 1998*, New York/Oxford, Oxford University Press.

VandePitte, M. *et al.* (1994) *NGO's - missionarissen van de nieuwe kolonisatie?*, Berchem, EPO VZW.

Van der Velden, F. (1980) *Ontwikkelingssamenwerking vanuit West-Europa met India; Drie case studies*, Nijmegen, Third World Centre, Catholic University Nijmegen.

Van der Velden, F. (1988) 'Tijgerweduwen, landlozen, schizofrenen en voddenrapers; Nederlandse medefinancieringsprojecten in India', in: *Derde Wereld*, vol. 7, no. 2, pp. 7-29.

Van der Velden, F. (1992) Mag het ietsje minder zijn? Een andere visie op de LIW-campagne 'Werk tegen Armoede', in: *India Nu*, March-April.

Van der Velden, F. (1993) De Landelijke India Werkgroep: van solidariteit naar paternalisme, in: *Derde Wereld*, Vol. 12, No. 2, pp. 4-9.

Van der Velden, F. (1994a) Tien dilemma's bij particuliere ontwikkelingssamenwerking, in: *Derde Wereld*, vol. 12, no. 4, pp. 2-24.

Van der Velden, F. (1994b) Westerse donoren zijn niet meer de reddende engelen, in: *Trouw*, 3 november, p. 11.

Van der Velden, F. (1995) *Particuliere ontwikkelingssamenwerking op de helling*, Nijmegen, Third World Centre, Nijmegen Catholic

University (Occasional paper 43).

Van der Velden, F. (1996) *Some half-cooked ideas about sustainable partnership between NGDOs from the South and North*, Paper presented at the Partnership Consultation on Participatory Process, Calcutta, November.

Van der Velden, F. and J. Zweers (1997) Personele samenwerking; Beleid, resultaten en perspectieven, in: K. Lieten and F. van der Velden (eds.) (1997)), *Grenzen aan de hulp; beleid en effecten van ontwikkelingssamenwerking*, Amsterdam, Uitgeverij Het Spinhuis, pp. 245-269.

Van de Waal, T. (1987) 10 Jaar LIW : van Derde-Wereldgroep tot uitgeverij?, in: *India Nieuwsbrief*, No. 50, September-October.

Van de Werk, J.K. (1981) Nawoord bij Chinua Achebe 'Pijl van God', in: Ch. *Achebe, Pijl van God*, Amsterdam, Rainbow pocketboeken (first edition: 1964).

Van Nieuwenhuijze, C.A.O. (1984) Does development have anything to do with culture, in: C.A.O. van Nieuwenhuijze (ed.), *Development regardless of Culture? A series of Public Lectures at the Institute of Social Studies, Spring, 1983*, Leiden, E.J. Brill.

Van Nieuwenhuijze, C.A.O. (1993) Cultuur en ontwikkeling: modegril of keerpunt?, in: *Informatie Ontwikkelingssamenwerking*, No. 40, Den Haag, Ministerie van Buitenlandse Zaken.

Van Wichelen, S. (1978) Mythevorming rond het Nederlandse medefinancieringsprogramma, in: *Internationale Spectator*, September, pp. 552-560.

Vereecken B. and F. van Ooyen (1989) Interview with C. Oskam, in: *Internationale Samenwerking* June, pp. 12-15.

Wereld en Zending (1997) Thema nummer *Nieuwe expansie*, Kampen, Kok.

Wertheim, W. (1964) *East-West Paralells*, Den Haag, Van Hoeve.

Wertheim, W. (1971) *Evolutie en revolutie; De golfslag der emancipatie*, Amsterdam, Van Gennep.

Wertheim, W. (1997) *Third World whence and whither? Protective state versus agressive market*, Amsterdam, Spinhuis.

Wils, F. (1991) Medefinanciering en partnerorganisaties in de jaren negentig: mogelijkheden en bespreking van een operationele utopie, in: Ph. Quarles van Ufford and F. Wils, *Kwaliteitszorg in de jaren 1990*, Den Haag, Novib.

World Bank (1988) *Rural Development: World Bank Experience 1965 - 1986*, Washington D.C., World Bank.

World Bank (1990a) *Strengthening the Banks Work on Popular Participation*, Washington D.C., World Bank (mimeo).

World Bank (1990b) *World Development Report; Poverty*, Washington D.C., World Bank.

World Bank (1992) *World Development Report* : Oxford, World Bank/ Oxford University Press.

World Bank (1998) *Assessing Aid – what works, what doesn't, and why: a World Bank policy research report*, Oxford : Oxford University Press.

World Bank (2000) *India - policies to reduce poverty and accelerate sustainable development, Poverty Reduction and Economic Management Unit South Asia Region*, Report No. 19471-IN, January.

INDEX